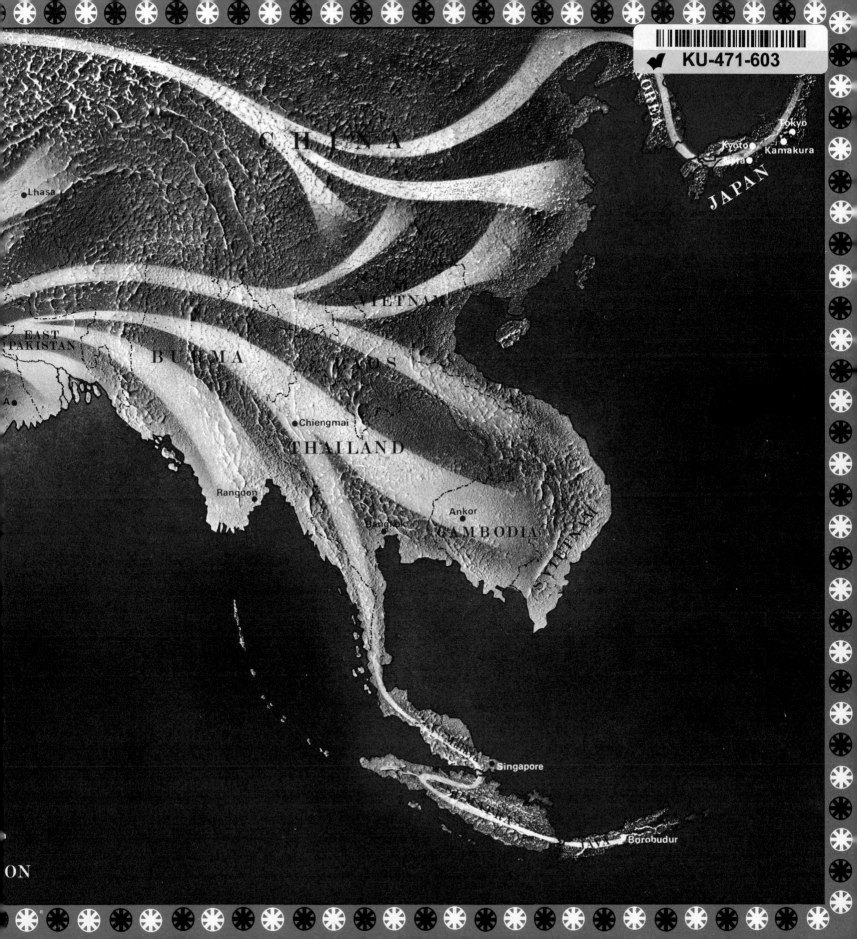

CHINA

Lhasa

EAST
PAKISTAN

BURMA

VIETNAM

LAOS

Chiengmai

THAILAND

Rangoon

Bangkok

Ankor

CAMBODIA

VIETNAM

KOREA

Tokyo

Kyoto
Kamakura

JAPAN

Singapore

JAVA
Borobudur

ON

BUDDHA

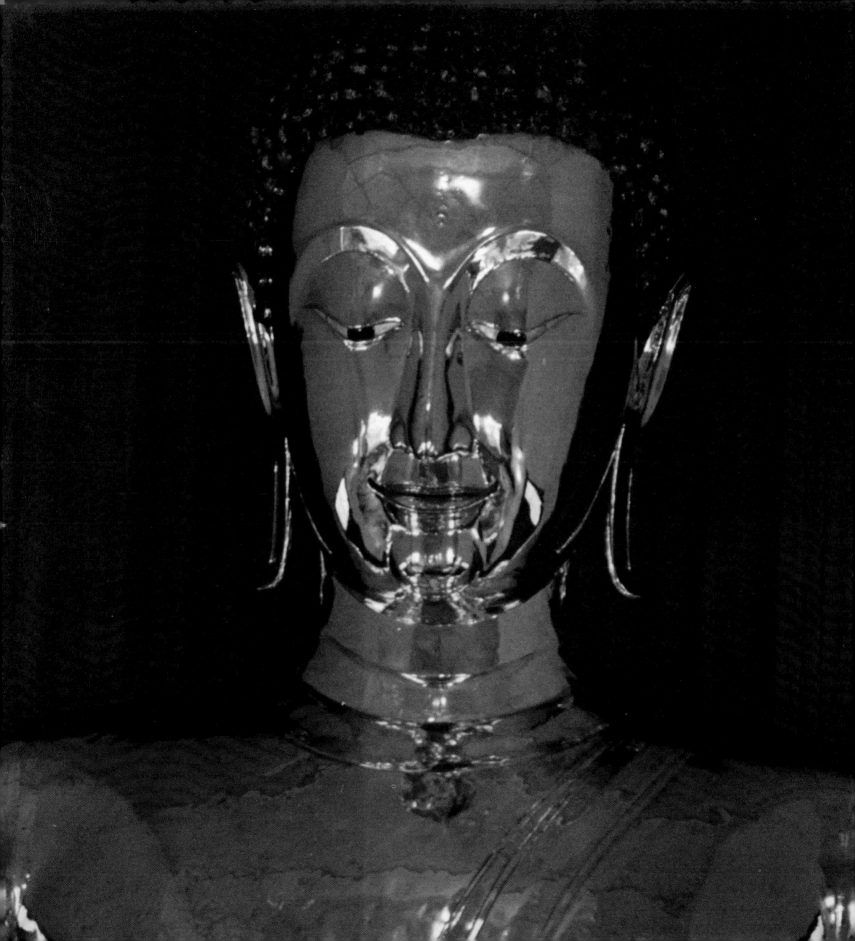

BUDDHA

WILLIAM MACQUITTY

NELSON

ACKNOWLEDGEMENTS

I wish to acknowledge with grateful thanks the help so generously given to me over the past forty years by Buddhists in all parts of the world. I am also greatly honoured by the foreword that His Holiness the Dalai Lama has so graciously written, and for the guidance given to me by distinguished leaders of Buddhism, including the head of the Zen order in Kyoto, Zenkei Shibayama; all of which has made the creation of this book a very great pleasure. Finally I wish to thank John Lowry of the Victoria and Albert Museum, London, whose deep knowledge of Buddhism and keen delight in this subject have been a source of invaluable information and assistance.

End-paper map by Vernon Mills. The scale of the map has been modified for diagrammatic purposes and is not intended to be geographically accurate.

Standing figure of the Lord Buddha; bronze. Found at Sultanganj, India. About sixth century A.D.

Thomas Nelson and Sons Ltd
36 Park Street London W1
P.O. Box 336 Apapa Lagos
P.O. Box 25012 Nairobi
P.O. Box 21149 Dar es Salaam
P.O. Box 2187 Accra
77 Coffee Street San Fernando Trinidad
Thomas Nelson (Australia) Ltd
597 Little Collins Street Melbourne 3000
Thomas Nelson and Sons (South Africa)
  (Proprietary) Ltd
51 Commissioner Street Johannesburg
Thomas Nelson and Sons (Canada) Ltd
81 Curlew Drive Don Mills Ontario

17 141071 8

First Published 1969

© William MacQuitty 1969

Phototypeset by
Oliver Burridge Filmsetting Ltd, Crawley, Sussex

Printed and Bound in Italy by
Arnoldo Mondadori, Verona

Frontispiece
This beautiful image of Buddha weighing over five tons was cast in solid gold in the 13th century; it now rests in Wat Trimitr, Bangkok.

FOREWORD

This book contains a simple and lucid account of the life and doctrine of Gautama Buddha. It shows how His teaching has sustained the ever growing number of His followers for over two thousand years and how its wisdom has encompassed everything that modern thought can devise. As the book traces the spreading of the doctrine from country to country each area is beautifully illustrated with the author's pictures of the magnificent works of art which the philosophy of Buddha inspired.

Today the fate of the world depends on the tolerance and goodwill of its nations. History has provided innumerable examples of the terrible results of greed and power, but man has failed to learn from the lessons of the past. It is my sincere hope that this book may remove some of the barriers of fear and hatred that divide the world and restore charity and compassion to mankind. I also hope that it will help to contribute towards the achievement of a closer and better understanding among the major, different religions of the world.

THE DALAI LAMA

Swarg Ashram
DHARMSALA CANTT.
Kangra/H.P.
INDIA.

TO

The Compassionate

The Buddha Shakyamuni as an ascetic, his body emaciated by the abstinences which he underwent in an unsuccessful attempt to achieve enlightenment. A stone sculpture from Gandhara, West Pakistan, second to fourth century A.D.

THE DART OF LIFE

The dart of life hits the spinning earth. Instantly the newborn child receives the gift of colour, race and creed, and in the first few years these become set into a rigid pattern under the pressures of parents, Church and State. By such accidents of birth the fate of human beings is decided, their opinions formed, their beliefs prescribed, until it is wellnigh impossible for the hard shell of prejudice to be broken.

In the beginning, man was a lonely, hungry animal; his strongest instinct was self-preservation. Over the years he multiplied enormously and developed social feelings which brought him to live with his fellows as a tribe. Property and enslavement followed, protection was bought by goods or service. Today, the State promises security in this world; the Church promises salvation in the next. Primitive and to some extent sophisticated religions deal in fear of the unknown; all offer some form of spiritual protection now and in the life hereafter, some reassurance to the frightened traveller on the dangerous journey of life that he is not alone, but that an all-powerful being is watching over him.

Innumerable religions have sprung from man's desperate need for security; all have powerful beings who can be wooed into helping the unhappy mortal. Some have one god, others many. Against this welter of conflicting mysteries there stands a teaching that has no god, but confines itself to the qualities required for the journey of life and its inevitable end. Although it does not actively seek followers it already has some 300 million and the number is growing daily. This teaching was propounded five centuries before Christ by a man, Siddhartha Gautama, later known as Buddha, The Enlightened One.

From his birthplace in north-east India the words of Gautama have brought comfort and happiness to many countries and to people of widely varying sects and creeds. H. G. Wells says in his *Outline of History*:

> 'There was much in the real teaching of Jesus that a rich man or a priest or a trader or an imperial official or any ordinary respectable citizen could not accept without the most revolutionary changes in his way of living, yet there was nothing that a follower of the actual teaching of Gautama Sakya might not receive very readily, nothing to prevent a primitive Buddhist from being also a Nazarene, and nothing to prevent a personal disciple of Jesus from accepting all the recorded teachings of Buddha.'

Gautama was a man, not a god, and his teaching a philosophy

Above
It was foretold that Buddha's mother, Maya, would dream that a white elephant would enter her right side and, in consequence, she would conceive and bear a child who was to become the historical Buddha Shakyamuni.

Below
The Lord Buddha was born in a small park called the Lumbini garden. Unlike ordinary mortals, he came out of his mother's right side while she stood and held on to the branch of a tree.

rather than a religion. He did not create a centrally organized establishment nor did he teach a doctrine absolutely binding on all believers. His ideas were not restricted by dogma and his doctrine therefore flourished in a wide variety of schools, each naturally regarding their own interpretation as the correct one. In each new area into which it spread, Buddhism absorbed part of the local religion and art, but it also broke the bonds of social behaviour and unlocked the gateway to new realms of thought, enabling the people it liberated to produce some of the finest creative work the world has ever seen.

In order to understand the appeal of Gautama's solution to the mystery of life we must go back to the beginning of man in the vast subcontinent of India. Here was a country isolated from the rest of the world by great oceans and enormous mountain ranges; its climate varying between the burning heat of the plains and the everlasting snows of the Himalayas. Here too were fertile valleys and mighty rivers. The earliest inhabitants worshipped nature. Trees – rare in the plains – lent shade from the scorching sun; rivers and pools supplied life-giving water and so became sacred. Animals and birds, the monkeys that chattered in the sacred trees, the gay peacocks and the venomous snakes that settled there, were looked upon as gods because in some respects they could outstrip mankind. They are still venerated today, not only the wild creatures but also the tame; and the cow that gives milk and butter for the nourishment of man and dung for his fire, walks in sacred freedom through the busy streets of Delhi and Calcutta.

India is a country where the ancient traditions, in spite of numerous invasions, remain almost unchanged with the passage of time. The worship of animals still flourishes alongside the use of nuclear power.

The first people to enter the country were probably Negroid, related to the aborigines of Ceylon, Sumatra and possibly Australia. These were soon followed by Dravidians and later Mongoloid races. Invasion followed invasion, horde after horde of fierce Aryan peoples poured through the north-western passes to mingle with those already there. But bloody conquest, rape and slavery did not destroy the original races and today traces of each can still be seen. Aboriginal tribes – Santals, Bhils and Gonds – survive in the hills and continue to believe in the oldest form of Animism. They do not believe in a soul or the hereafter. Their lives are here and now, the animals they worship are not spirits: if they swear on a tiger skin they believe that, if they speak falsely, a real tiger will eat them.

The basic religion today is Hinduism, which is perhaps more a social code than a religion. Hindus believe in the Universal or Supreme Soul represented by a trinity of gods: Brahma, the Omnipresent One, is the Father of the Hindu trinity – the Creator; Vishnu the Preserver is the second member, who constantly wars against the third, Shiva the Destroyer. Shiva also has another aspect: generative power signified by the sacred bull Nandi and by the phallic emblem the Lingam. Together they account for the creation, preservation and

A crude image covered with red ochre under this tree in India shows that it is being worshipped. More precisely, it is probable that it is the spirit who lives in the tree, or the protective deity of the village, who have been induced to enter into it, who are being worshipped. Tree-worship is found in many countries and is widespread in India today. It certainly goes back to pre-Buddhist times and was, in all likelihood, absorbed into Buddhism. This may account for the story of Buddha finding his enlightenment under a tree, and for the use of a tree as a symbol for him.

A Buddhist worshipper in the Temple of the Tooth, Kandy, Ceylon, making an offering of a flower. In most Buddhist countries an act of devotion includes making offerings of flowers, fruit (or other food such as rice), burning incense, or placing a small square of gold-leaf on an image of the deity being worshipped. Usually devotional activity is not congregational but is made by individuals. Their worship is personal and direct without the intercession of monks or priests. This enables the worshipper to cultivate a close and vital relationship between himself and the deity he worships.

destruction of the universe and all that it contains. Individual souls are simply different manifestations of the Supreme Soul into which, ultimately, they must merge, but before they can do this, they must work out their destinies by passing through a series of births.

The priests soon found Brahma too colourless and abstract for their flock: he could awaken little sympathy for those accustomed to worshipping the sacrifice of flesh and blood. Female consorts were found for the Hindu Trinity. Sarasvati, the goddess of speech and learning, became the consort of Brahma. Shri or Lakshmi, the goddess of beauty and fortune, the consort of Vishnu, and Uma or Parvati, the daughter of Himavat, the god of the Himalayas, that of Shiva. She had other names: Kali the Black One, Durga the Terrible One and Mahadevi the Great Goddess.

These gods demanded sacrifices, perhaps the most spectacular of which was the horse sacrifice, a ritual that was designed to confer universal sovereignty on the king and ensure prosperity for his kingdom and his people. A number of the king's warriors, including, where practicable, his son, followed a fine stallion round the perimeter of the kingdom. The ground it covered was considered to belong to the king – a concept reinforced by the warriors. When it returned to its starting-point, it was smothered, and as many as 600 horses had their throats cut whilst the king's wives paid homage to the smothered stallion, no doubt to ensure their own fertility and that of their master. Today sacrifices are still made in India, and in Calcutta the black goddess Kali claims her victims.

From its beginning about 1500 B.C. Hinduism accepted almost any beliefs, atheism, pantheism or monotheism, but its real strength lay in its caste system. In its earliest form caste may have sprung from

Above and below
Yashodhara prepares for her marriage with Gautama. One of a series of sculptured reliefs, showing the life of the Buddha, surrounding the base of the relic mound at Borabadhur, Java. About A.D. 800.
Left
The Bodhisattva Gautama, riding his horse Kanthaka, leaves his family to take up the homeless life; stone. India, Amaravati period, second to third century A.D.

Below
The attack of the evil forces of Mara. This panel was carved before figures of the Buddha were shown in sculpture. Here, instead, he is represented by his throne. Amarvati, India, about second century A.D.

the religious tradition of veneration of the elders – the mother teaching her children to obey the head of the family, the father's tools and weapons being regarded as sacred. It may also have been looked upon as a means of protecting the succession in a noble family. A wealthy man realized that with the protection of caste he could place himself and his family in a different category from the poor. There would be no point in overthrowing him if it were plain that his son would automatically take his place. The protected conditions of the Ganges Valley, remote from the winds of change of the outside world, confirmed this pattern of privilege over the years. Indian society was divided into four main groups. At the top were the Brahmans, the priests and teachers; second came the Kahatryas, the warriors; third the Vaishyas, herdsmen, merchants, landowners and moneylenders; and lastly the Sudras, the workers. They were governed by rules which were strict to the point of extremity. Persons of one caste could neither intermarry nor even eat with members of another. Caste also meant, with few exceptions, that the child had to follow the father's trade. Over the years innumerable sub-castes have been created, so that today, below the exalted Brahmans, the twice born, there are more than 2,000 castes arranged in descending order, all with their special rules and requirements.

The self-exaltation of the Brahman caste was not altogether due to priestly arrogance and ambition. To the Brahman, nature represented a continuous scale running from the lowest to the highest – himself. It seemed to the Brahman a reasonable supposition. There must be order in the universe and such order would naturally run from low to high, from the lowest degradation to the absolute purity of the supreme spirit. The suffering and hardships which beset the lower orders would eventually pave the way for them to advance to the next stage.

But whilst many Brahmans were worthy of the respect with which they were treated, and whilst undoubtedly many sought unswervingly for the mastery over their senses which would lead them to personal salvation, none had compassion for their less fortunate fellow men. Below the innumerable castes lay the wretched untouchables – the outcasts whose occupations for the general welfare of the community, oddly enough, placed them beyond the pale. Butchers, fishermen, undertakers, cleaners, sweepers, all came into this class; and if for breaking some petty rule a man lost caste, then he did not descend to the caste immediately beneath him but became an outcast. These unfortunates had to live in isolated quarters and to be most careful to avoid polluting all the members of the castes. The fear of defilement was so strong that even if the shadow of an untouchable fell upon the member of a caste he was obliged to carry out rites of purification. The human outcast, for his part, was even more terrified of causing such a defilement since, apart from the thrashing he might receive, he believed that he would be reborn in the body of an animal.

Down the ages the system has had many formidable opponents,

13

Left
In a temple at Bodh Gaya a
monk summons his brother
monks to worship.
Right
Monks preparing some of
the many butter lamps used
in a ceremony in the temple
at Bodh Gaya, India.

from Gautama to Gandhi, but it has survived all attacks. In spite of the endeavours of the enlightened Indian government, the sweeper is still an outcast in the eyes of the community and performs his necessary function as inconspicuously as possible.

Thus, in this world of castes and outcasts, gods, goddesses and their accompanying priestly rituals, the stage was set for the arrival of a new leader whose philosophy was to cut through the ignorance and superstition which clouded the minds of the masses of India.

GAUTAMA

Gautama, according to the accounts of the time, was born into this world of complex religious beliefs about the year 563 B.C. His father was the Raja of the Shakya clan, whose land was in the foothills of the Himalayas, and was classed by the Brahmans as a Kshatriya, a member of the warrior caste. He was an Aryan. Gautama was the family name and Siddhartha was the child's personal name. The capital of his father's state was Kapilavastu and it was on a journey from there that his mother Maya gave birth to him in the Lumbini Gardens in Nepal, still a shrine to his memory.

As the child grew to manhood, he was surrounded by all the luxury and attention still given to a male heir in one of the Indian states today. His needs were satisfied almost before they arose; he was bathed, dried and dressed by attendants. He was good-looking and athletic; hunting and love-making, feasting and dancing, music and discourse filled his days. The palace gardens with fountains and exotic scents surrounded him. Peacocks strutted among the jasmin and the temple flowers. His pleasure-girls lay in their perfumed pavilions, waiting their lord's command.

When he was nineteen he was married to a beautiful girl, Yashodhara, and it seemed that life had given him all that anyone could have wished, but Gautama was unsatisfied. There is no evidence that there was any literature at that time; the only learning was a monopoly of the Brahmans and this was limited to the memorizing and endless repetition of the Vedas. Gautama had a fine brain and wanted to use it. The unlimited gratification of the senses began to pall; he longed for something, but what?

While he was thus troubled by the futility of his existence, four

16

Above
Although the Buddha is often described as the son of a king, and therefore a prince, it is probable that he was born into the family of a ruler of lesser rank than a king. In this first century B.C. sculpture from Barhut, his family life is shown, but he is represented by a wheel hung with a garland of foliage.

Below
One day a girl who had been converted to Buddhism, but whose parents were Jainas, created a scene in the street and disgraced her mother and father. She prayed to the Buddha, who came and saved her from severe punishment. In this stone sculpture from Gandhara, West Pakistan, she can be seen bowing down at the Buddha's feet.

Above

The Lord Buddha preaching in the Deer Park, near Benares. This incident is often described as his 'turning the Wheel of the Law' and is symbolized by the wheel below his throne. Listening are comrades who once deserted him, the god Indra and princes. Stone sculpture from Gandhara, West Pakistan.

Above right

This stone sculpture from Gandhara shows the Lord Buddha about to call the earth to witness that he had given alms. Just before this incident he had resisted the temptations offered by the daughters of the evil King Mara and an attack by his army (symbolized by fallen soldiers under his throne). Now, gods, men and beasts assemble to be present at his enlightenment.

events occurred which convinced him that he must change his way of life. While his father had surrounded him with all the luxuries of India he had kept from him the sad realities of life. Gautama fretted at this luxurious captivity and persuaded his father to let him drive through the capital.

On the appointed day Channa, his loyal coachman, drove his prince through the city in the royal chariot drawn by four white horses. They passed through streets lined with cheering subjects and on into the country with its pastures and pleasant trees. Here the Prince saw by the roadside an old man bent and feeble with age. 'Who is this?' he asked. 'Why is his body withered, his eyes bleared — he can hardly support himself with his staff.'

The good Channa, warned by Gautama's father against exposing the prince too freely to the harshness of life outside the palace, was embarrassed and hardly dared to answer the truth. Finally he said, 'These are the symptoms of old age. This same man was once a youth full of life and energy, but now, as the years have passed, his beauty is gone and the strength of his life is wasted.'

Siddhartha was greatly affected by the words of his charioteer. 'What joy or pleasure can men take,' he thought to himself, 'when they know that they must soon wither and pine away?'

Further on they came upon a sick man by the wayside, his body disfigured and convulsed, groaning with pain.

The prince asked his charioteer: 'What kind of man is this?' And the charioteer replied: 'This man is sick, his body is out of order. We are all subject to such conditions: the poor and the rich, the ignorant and the wise, all creatures that have bodies are liable to disease.'

Siddhartha was still more moved.

The charioteer urged on the horses to escape the dreary sight when suddenly they stopped.

Four people were passing, carrying a corpse. The prince, shuddering at the sight of a lifeless body, asked the charioteer: 'What is this they carry? There are streamers and flower garlands; but the

A few of the 1,000 figures of Kan-non (Avalokiteshvara) in the Sanjusangendo ('Hall of 33 Spaces'), Kyoto. It was originally built in the twelfth century by a pious emperor who hoped, by doing so, to bring peace to his realm.

18

men that follow are overwhelmed with grief!' The charioteer replied: 'That is a dead man. His body is stiff; his life is gone; his thoughts are still; his family and the friends who loved him now carry his corpse to the grave.'

The prince was filled with awe and horror. 'Is this the only dead man,' he asked, 'or does the world contain more instances?'

With a heavy heart the charioteer replied: 'All over the world it is the same. He who begins life must end it. There is no escape from death.'

Deeply moved by this revelation the prince exclaimed: 'O wordly men! How fatal is your delusion! Inevitably your body will crumble into dust, yet carelessly, unheedingly, you live on.'

Gautama's thoughts were plagued by the insecurity of his position. Of what avail were the pleasure gardens, the luxurious life, if disease or death could strike at any moment or, failing that, old age inevitably remove the joys of living? He became more determined than ever to find a way to resolve the futility of his existence.

As they drove back to the palace through the cool of the evening, they saw an ascetic with shaven head and yellow robe. There are many such men still to be found in India who find no satisfaction in material things and give up the comfort of the family hearth to seek some deeper reality. Gautama resolved to adopt the homeless life and to search for the answer to the tragedies that he had just seen.

As they entered the city, a maiden named Kisa Gotami, struck by the beauty and noble bearing of Gautama, sang: 'Happy the father that begot you, happy the mother that nursed you, happy the wife that calls husband this lord so glorious.' The prince, hearing this greeting, replied: 'Happy are they who have found deliverance. Longing for peace of mind, I shall seek the bliss of Nirvana.'

As Gautama entered the palace news was brought to him that Yosodhara had borne him a son. Arrangements were made for a great banquet to celebrate the birth of his heir. Saddened at the thought that here was yet another tie to break, Gautama sought solitude. Late that night he awoke in great agony of spirit, convinced that he must save not only himself but all mankind from the world of suffering. Dressing himself quietly he picked his way through the sleeping forms of his pleasure-girls and told the faithful Channa to saddle his horse Kanthaka. Then he went to his wife's room and saw her sleeping softly surrounded by garlands of scented flowers, his baby son in her arms. He longed to hold his son but was afraid of wakening his wife, and so, greatly sorrowing, he at last turned away and walked quietly through the moonlit garden to the spot where Channa waited with his horse.

As he rode through the night with Channa, Gautama's thoughts swayed between anguish at parting from his loved ones and the desire to help humanity find an answer to the impermanence of all earthly things. While he pondered, the voice of Mara, the Tempter of Mankind, spoke to him from the scented air. 'Turn back and thou

20

Above
The grief and despair of the mourners contrast sharply with the Buddha's expression of peace and contentment as he passes into Nirvana in this sculptured stone relief from Gandhara, West Pakistan, second to fourth century A.D.

Below
In the earliest Buddhist sculpture the Buddha himself was never represented. Instead, his presence was indicated by symbols. In this first century B.C. sculpture from Bharhut, showing his Mahaparinirvana, his place is taken by a *stupa* (relic mound).

Above

After the cremation of the Buddha's mortal remains, his ashes were divided into eight portions for distribution to the eight Buddhist kings. In this second to fourth century sculptured relief from Gandhara, West Pakistan, the Brahman Drona is distributing the relics; he has given one each to two kings, who stand each side, and holds another ready to give to one of the other kings who are waiting. The other five relics lie on the table.

shalt be king and I will make you ruler over all. You will have pleasure and contentment all your days. Abandon this path which will only lead you to destruction.' But Gautama refused to turn back and Mara said, 'Henceforth like your shadow I will follow you. Some day lust, cruelty or malice will betray you and I will know, and on that day you will be mine.'

The country they rode through was bathed in the light of the full moon. It was the month of June and Gautama was twenty-nine. They travelled far during the night and in the morning found themselves by the sandy shore of a small river at the boundary of the kingdom. Gautama dismounted and taking his sword cut off his long black hair and gave it to Channa with all his ornaments and jewels. Channa tried to dissuade his master from this terrible step, but Gautama told him not to grieve over their parting. 'All living things must part. Let us do so now of our own accord; in due course death would tear us apart and we would have no say in the matter.' Broken-hearted the loyal Channa left his master and returned to the palace.

Gautama continued on foot and presently met a beggar with whom he exchanged clothes. Now, divested of all his precious possessions, he was at last free to pursue his search for wisdom. As he walked along he recalled the song of the maiden Kisa Gotami. Alas, what permanence was there in her happiness.

Gradually he made his way southwards until he came to a grove of trees where the great sage Alara Kalama lived. Here Gautama sat at the feet of the holy man and listened to his teaching. 'The five senses,' he was told, 'are perceived by the soul. The soul is the I that feels, the I that smells, the I that tastes, the I that sees and the I that hears. The I is the soul and unless you believe this there is no way to salvation.' But Gautama found no comfort in this unquestioning belief.

He then went to another sage, Uddaka Ramaputta, who taught that men differed in possessions, in quality and in their wordly position because of their karma. They inherited from former existences the effect of their past actions: good deeds produced good effects, evil the reverse. Gautama accepted the law of cause and effect in nature, the present reaping what the past has sown, but whilst he did not deny the possibility of a soul, he did not find any evidence to support the idea of an eternal being, of a self which remains the same but migrates from body to body throughout the ages. The continuity of man he likened to the lighting of one candle from another. The candle is different but the flame is continuous. We hold a similar notion when the Olympic flame is carried by many runners across the world to light the Games. It is the original flame from Mount Olympus passed on from torch to torch until at last it reaches its destination, but the extinct torches have no further part to play.

Gautama then went to the priests in the temples, but his gentle mind was repelled by the cruelty of their blood sacrifices. What sort of people were these who thought that unnecessary cruelty performed on the altars of the gods could atone for their own wickedness? How

Above
A group of Thai monks look out from
their monastery across the countryside. A
buddhist monk leaves his home and takes up
a life of abstinence and chastity. After a
period as a novice, which can be ended
whenever he likes, he is ordained at a
ceremony during which he promises to obey
the rules of the order. Unlike Christian
ministers, however, this neither qualifies
him to take charge of souls nor to intercede
on behalf of the laity. He takes part in the
routine work of the monastery, studies and
teaches, not only the Way of the Law but
also secular subjects such as reading and
writing.
Right
Offerings left by worshippers of Kuan-yin in
the Phor Kark See Temple, Singapore, to give
them protection against misfortune in this life
and escape from rebirth in the next.

could the slaughter of innocent victims take away the sins of mankind?

Gautama continued his search for truth and presently came upon a group of five ascetics who lived in the jungle of Uruvela, near Rajgir. These men lived a life of the utmost austerity, practising rigorous self-discipline and striving to subdue their passions. Gautama admired their way of life and joined them. For the next six years he patiently trained his body and mind in the most rigorous forms of ascetic hardship. The enthusiasm with which he approached this new life so impressed the five that they came to regard him as their master, but Gautama was unsatisfied. His body was wasted from constant fasting and the fame of his holiness drew people from all around to seek his blessing, but he was no nearer to the truth which he sought. Mortification had not extinguished his desires nor did enlightenment come from meditation.

Gautama saw that he had become so weak that he was unable to think clearly and decided to strengthen himself with food and drink. While he was reaching this conclusion he collapsed on the ground and the five ascetics thought him dead. Fortunately a herdsman's daughter named Nanda was passing and gave him milk which revived him. Gautama now began to take food, but his disciples were filled with suspicion and thought that their master had given up his original high purpose. Seeing their lack of faith, Gautama decided to leave them and to continue his lonely search for truth, but the five were sceptical and reasoned that he was leaving them to seek a more comfortable life.

THE DAWNING

The dawning light of truth had been slow in coming, but realization was near at hand. Suppressing his grief at the lack of confidence displayed by his five disciples, Gautama wandered on alone until he came to a Bodhi tree at a place that is now known as Bodh Gaya near Benares. It was the night of the full moon in May and he was thirty-five. As he sat down to rest under the spreading branches of the tree, he once again heard the voice of his old enemy Mara tempting him and calling up his evil hosts to attack the steadfastness of his purpose. In the colourful language of the Sanskrit Gospel, the forces of darkness were powerless against Gautama: 'The flames of hell became whole-

Right
The Buddhist cave-temples of Ajanta, India. These were carved out of the living rock mainly during the fifth and sixth centuries A.D. They are adorned with some of the finest early Indian sculpture and painting.

Below
The Buddha about to step down from his seat in front of a formalized burial mound in a rock-cut assembly hall in Cave XXVI, Ajanta. First half of the seventh century A.D.

some breezes of perfume and the angry thunderbolts were changed into lotus blossoms. As the rays of the sun drown the darkness of the world, so he who perseveres in his search will find truth and the truth will enlighten him.'

Having thus resisted the voice of temptation Gautama gave himself up to meditation. Pondering on the origin of birth and death he recognized that ignorance was the root of all evil. The cause of sorrow is hidden in the ignorance from which life grows – the child is born a savage. If men could only see the results of selfishness they would turn away from it, but selfhood blinds them and they cling to their desires. The path to freedom and peace is the extinction of self. The truth that Gautama had perceived was that if man places himself in the centre of his life, if all life is regarded from his own selfish stand-point, then he is doomed to suffer.

With the realization of this fundamental truth Gautama attained enlightenment, and so became Buddha, the Enlightened One, although indeed there is no record that he ever referred to himself by this title. After resting for some days he set out for Benares, where his five disciples were still living in austerity. They greeted him coldly; he was the one who had taken food, the one who had failed them. For several days he reasoned with them and finally they were convinced that he had gained enlightenment and hailed him as the Buddha. There in the Deer Park of Isipatana at Sarnath near Benares the Buddha revealed his doctrine, in the form of a sermon. Once more it

Left
Yama, the god of death, was originally
a Hindu deity whose origin could
probably be traced to primitive beliefs
long before he was mentioned in the
puranas. In Tibetan Buddhism, as can
be seen in this bronze image, he has
acquired many attributes symbolizing
ideas introduced by Tantric beliefs.

Right
The desire for maternal protection and
the obvious example of women as
symbols of creation have resulted, in
many primitive societies, in the worship
of a mother goddess. In Northern
Buddhism this has expressed itself in
the rise of the cult of the 'White Tara'
and her enormous popularity in Tibet
and Nepal.

was the night of the full moon, and just three months after his enlightenment.

This sermon, known later as 'Setting in Motion the Wheel of Righteousness', is found in all of the Buddhist scriptures, with little variation. Gautama spoke of the two extremes that had moulded his life up to the time of his enlightenment: the early period of sensuous luxury where every desire was gratified and even encouraged; then the long weary years of absolute austerity and mortification of the body until thought was no longer possible. Between these two extremes lay the middle path where reason held sway, together with goodwill to all sentient beings.

So that it might be more easily spread by word of mouth, Gautama gave his teaching a numerical framework. He called it the Four Noble Truths and the Eightfold Path which leads to the end of suffering.

His first Noble Truth was the existence of sorrow and suffering. Birth is painful, sickness is painful, old age is painful, death is painful. Craving that cannot be satisfied is painful: it is sad to be joined to that which we do not like and sadder still to be parted from those we love.

The second Noble Truth was the cause of suffering. This is wrongly directed desire: the selfish personal craving of mankind for material wealth, for the gratification of the senses, for immortality. The craving for selfish enjoyment entangles men in a mesh of sorrow.

The third Noble Truth was that sorrow, pain, illness and suffering can be ended. The man who conquers himself, who overcomes his own desires, who liberates himself from the tyranny of his ego occupying the centre of his private thoughts, becomes free. He reaches the higher wisdom, Nirvana, serenity of soul.

The fourth Noble Truth was the means to the end of suffering. This is the Eightfold Path. The wise man will follow this path and make an end of sorrow.

The Eightfold Path consists of the following:

1 *Right Views* There is no room for lazy thinking, superstition has no place – only truth can be accepted. Gautama condemned the current belief in the transmigration of souls, or indeed in an enduring personal soul.

2 *Right Intentions* Gautama did not teach the extinction of desire but the change of desire from selfish cravings to the desire to help others, desire for justice, desire for truth and the love of one's neighbour.

3 *Right Speech* Refraining from false and malicious speech.

4 *Right Conduct* Refraining from taking life or taking what is not given.

5 *Right Livelihood* The right way of earning a living.

6 *Right Effort* Good intentions were not enough. The disciple had to be keenly critical of his actions.

Above
Figures of the Buddha with celestial attendants carved from the rock façade of one of the Ajanta caves. First half of the seventh century A.D.

Above right
Chapel of Hariti, Cave II, Ajanta, showing Hariti (*l*) and Panchika (*r*). Hariti was a demoness who became converted to Buddhism by the Lord Buddha. Panchika was her husband.

7 *Right Thoughts or Mindfulness* Awareness of the fundamental truths. The follower must always be on guard against feelings of self-satisfaction about his achievements.

8 *The Right State of a Peaceful Mind* Right concentration on the realities of truth and love of mankind and avoidance of the pointless ecstacies and witless euphoria of the devout that appear so often in religious rituals.

It says much for the soundness of these precepts that although they were spoken five centuries before Christ they contain much of the essential thought of every philosophy and every religion that the world has considered to be of value up to the present day.

Gautama demanded keen application of these principles from his disciples. He would tolerate no unfulfilled good intentions, no halfhearted efforts. Here was a religion that differed from any other religion up to that time. It was a way of life and conduct, not a religion of ritual and sacrifice. It had no theology, no sacred order of priests, nor did it seek to alter belief in the innumerable gods that were worshipped in India.

The fundamental teaching of Buddha is clear and simple. The suffering and miseries of humanity are due to insatiable selfishness, to the unlimited craving for personal satisfaction. Until man overcomes these desires his life is filled with trouble and his end is sorrow. There are many forms of craving: the desire for personal immortality;

Left
The 'White Tara' is sometimes called the 'Saviouress' or the 'Goddess with the Seven Eyes' (because she also has eyes on the soles of her feet, the palms of her hands, and one in the centre of her forehead). She is also regarded as having been the Chinese queen of a Tibetan king who lived in the seventh century A.D.
Right
As well as 'Saviouresses' such as the White Tara, Northern Buddhism has fierce female deities such as this Dakini who wage ceaseless war against the enemies of religion.

the desire for wordly goods; the desire for power. All these must be overcome before man can achieve serenity. The achievement of this high wisdom or Nirvana does not mean the extinction of man but the extinction of his own selfish ambitions and aims which inevitably make life a burden and a small and pitiful affair. The history of the world gives ample proof of the wisdom of the doctrine. The slow advancement of mankind has been achieved by unselfish actions, as Gautama taught. There can be no peace, no security, no social order unless men lose themselves in something greater than themselves. The gradual rise of humanity is on the shoulders of those who have gone before; their contribution, be it good or evil, becomes part of the whole heritage.

A cobra protects another from the heat of the sun by shading it with its outspread hood. In the same way the serpent king Muchilinda protected the Buddha from the rain while he was meditating during the sixth week after his enlightenment.

THE LIGHT

The Light spread slowly. From the first the teachings of Gautama were misunderstood. The removing of self from the centre of a person's life was taken to mean the renouncing of life itself, not difficult in a country where the intense heat made work unpleasant. Withdrawal

The Buddha seated in the position called 'turning the wheel of the law'. A carving from the front of one of the caves at Ajanta, early seventh century A.D.

from life was simpler and more attractive than hard work, and asceticism had always appealed to the Indian mind.

It was also considered necessary for the Master to be a person of public consequence, a man with whose fame and miraculous gifts disciples might the more easily impress the outer world and thus find alms for their livelihood. Even before his death the simple teaching of Gautama became overlaid with miracles attributed to him and the profoundly human man himself turned into a god who alone could give salvation to the world, when his real message was that everyone must discover the truth for himself. Over-enthusiastic disciples presented the Buddha as a saviour who could protect his followers from the torments of the hereafter and the possibility of rebirth as an animal. There were some who recognized the simple truth that Gautama had discovered, but their voices were drowned in the flood of euphoria that swept the new teaching in ever-widening circles throughout India.

Wonder grew upon wonder, and as time went on the followers, at heart simple and devout people, found themselves more and more enmeshed in the success of their own propaganda. Nothing was impossible, nothing too magnificent for their master. Even his birth became miraculous. The following passage is to be found in the *Buddhist Scriptures*:

'He [Gautama] came out of his mother's side, without causing her pain or injury. His birth was as miraculous as that of Aurva, Prithu, Mandhatri and Kakshivat, heroes of old who were born respectively from thigh, hand, the head or the armpit. So he issued from his mother's womb as befits a Buddha. He did not enter the world in the usual manner, and he appeared like one descended from the sky. And since he had for many aeons been engaged in the practice of meditation, he now was born in full awareness, and not thoughtless and bewildered as other people are. His limbs shone with the radiant hue of precious gold and lit up the space all around. Instantly he walked seven steps, firmly and with long strides.'*

Until his death forty-five years later, Gautama taught throughout north-east India. His teachings did not attack the current Brahmanism, there was no attempt to force conversion on people of other faiths nor has there ever been during the long history of Gautama's teaching up to the present day. The only conquest in the Buddhist view is the conquest of self. As Gautama pointed out again and again, the attainment of Truth is possible only when an immortal self is recognized as an illusion. Righteousness can be practised only when we have freed our mind from the passions of egotism. Perfect peace can dwell only where all vanity has disappeared.

Gradually the number of followers grew until it was impossible for Gautama to attend to them all. He therefore called his disciples

* *Buddhist Scriptures*, translated by Edward Conze (Penguin Classics), p. 35.

A drummer in the orchestra of Bodnath Temple in Nepal.

The Chini Lama, head of the Tibetan church in Nepal, invokes a deity with the aid of a bell and a drum made of two human skulls.

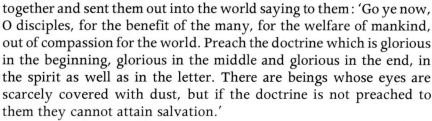

together and sent them out into the world saying to them: 'Go ye now, O disciples, for the benefit of the many, for the welfare of mankind, out of compassion for the world. Preach the doctrine which is glorious in the beginning, glorious in the middle and glorious in the end, in the spirit as well as in the letter. There are beings whose eyes are scarcely covered with dust, but if the doctrine is not preached to them they cannot attain salvation.'

Gautama also gave his first missionaries permission to ordain those eager to receive his teaching provided they were worthy. It is told that the first lay member was a rich merchant of Benares, who in spite of great wealth was full of sorrow and distress. Gautama said, 'Here is no distress; here are no tribulations. Come to me and I will teach you the truth and the truth will dispel your sorrows.'

As he listened the merchant perceived the truth and was ashamed of his costly garments richly adorned with pearls and precious stones. Gautama, reading his thoughts, said: 'Though a person be ornamented with jewels, the heart may have conquered the senses. The outward form does not constitute religion or affect the mind. The body of an ascetic may wear rags while his mind is immersed in worldliness.

'A man that dwells in lonely woods and yet covets worldly vanities is a worldling, while the man in worldly garments may let his heart soar high to heavenly thoughts. There is no distinction between the hermit and the layman, if both have banished thought of self.'

The merchant felt that a lamp had been lighted in the darkness surrounding him and said, 'Glorious is the truth, O Lord! The Buddha, the Holy One, our Master, sets up what has been overturned; he

Above left
A pilgrim prays at the site of the Lord Buddha's enlightenment Bodh Gaya, India. It is believed that the Bo tree is a descendant of the one under which the Buddha sat during the night before his enlightenment. Bodh Gaya is an important place of pilgrimage for Buddhists of all sects.
Above
The Himalayas by moonlight, seen from Dharmsala, North India. Present refuge of the Dalai Lama and Tibetan refugees.

Bodh Gaya, India. Tent for Tibetan pilgrims pitched by the side of the Temple. It is painted with the prayer 'Om mani padme hum'.

reveals what has been hidden; he points out the way to the wanderer that has gone astray; he lights a lamp in the darkness so that all who have eyes to see can discern the things that surround them.

> 'I take refuge in the Buddha, our Lord,
> I take refuge in the teaching revealed by him,
> I take refuge in the Order which he has founded.'

This formula is still used today by millions of Buddhists.

Gautama also taught in parables. At Uruvela there lived a group of Jatilas, Brahman ascetics with matted hair, believers in Krishna and also worshippers of fire. Their chief was Kashyapa, who was renowned as an authority on religion, and he was envious of the Buddha. Gradually, however, he perceived the truth of Gautama's teaching and asked that he and his followers might join the order. To them Gautama preached his famous Fire Sermon.

> 'Everything O Jatilas is burning. The eye is burning, thoughts are burning, all the senses are burning. They are burning with the fire of lust. There is anger, there is ignorance, there is hatred and as long as the fire finds inflammable things upon which it can feed, so long will it burn, and there will be birth and death, decay, grief, lamentation, suffering, despair and sorrow. Considering this the disciple of Truth will see the four Truths and walk in the Noble Eightfold Path. He will divest himself of passion and become free. He will be delivered from selfishness and attain the blessed state of Nirvana.'

37

A gold Nepalese mask of Bhairava,
a diety popular with both Hindus
and Buddhists in Nepal.

Kashyapa became an ardent follower of Gautama, and together they went with many disciples to Rajgir, where Gautama preached a sermon on 'self' to King Bimbisara and his people.

'He who knows the nature of his self and understands how his senses act, finds no room for the "I" and thus he will attain peace unending. The world holds the thought of "I" and from this arises false apprehension.

'Ye that are slaves of the "I", that toil in service of self from morning to night, that live in constant fear of birth, old age, sickness and death, receive the good tidings that your cruel master exists not. Self is an error, an illusion, a dream. Open your eyes and awake. See things as they are and you will be comforted. He who is awake will no longer be afraid of nightmares. He who recognizes the nature of the rope that seemed to be a serpent ceases to tremble. He who has found that there is no "I" will let go all the lusts and desires of egotism.'

Gautama regarded self, the ego which says 'I am', as a collection of five skandhas or heaps: Feelings, Perceptions, Impulses and Emotions, the Body and Acts of Consciousness. These emotions, sensations, ideas, wishes, thoughts and memories together produce a character, but a character which changes from moment to moment. The self is not an eternal, unchanging entity living in everlasting immutability somewhere in the man, rather it is a bundle of constantly changing prejudices which make up this personality.

Once self is understood and removed from the centre of the person's life and consideration for others put in its place, death loses much of its terror. In Buddhist countries such as Thailand, Burma, Cambodia and Ceylon the people are among the happiest on earth; death has no terrors for them and their funeral ceremonies are full of gaiety and colour.

THE TEACHING

The teaching of Gautama continued until his death. No one was turned away. He gave his doctrine equally to kings and to beggars. Although he had some reservations regarding women, he started an order of nuns. The first to be ordained was Kisa Gotami, possibly the same Kisa Gotami who praised him when he entered the city of Kapilavastu. She had a little son who died, and hoping that Gautama in his wisdom

The Buddha preaching. One of the most famous statues of the Buddha, it was found at Sarnath, India, close to the site of the deer park where he preached his first sermon.

could bring the child back to life, she sought his help. Gautama told her to go and bring him mustard seed from a house in her village where no child had died. Kisa went off full of joy to fetch the seed, but soon found that death had called at every home. Realizing that Gautama in his compassion had sent her to learn the truth, she buried her son and returned to Gautama. He asked her if she had got the mustard seed and she replied, 'That work is done. Lord, grant me support.' Gautama accepted her and she became the first nun to wear the yellow robe.

Gautama's father Suddhodana Raja sent word that he wished to see his son. It was now some seven years since Gautama had ridden away from his family to seek the answer to the futility of his existence. As he approached Kapilavastu with a train of followers his father with his relatives and ministers came out of his palace to meet him. Suddhodana was overcome with joy at the appearance of his son, but was also sad that he would never be his heir.

'I would offer you my kingdom,' he said, 'but if I did, you would account it as ashes.' Gautama replied, 'I know that your heart is full of love for the son whom you have lost, but let this love embrace all your fellow beings and you will receive the Truth and the peace of Nirvana will enter your heart.' And his father's heart was lightened.

Yashodhara, learning of her husband's arrival, sent their little son Rahula to him telling him that his father had four great mines of wealth and to ask for his inheritance. Rahula went to his father and asked for his inheritance. Gautama turned to Shariputra, his principal disciple, saying: 'My son asks for his inheritance. I cannot give him perishable treasures that will bring cares and sorrows, but I can give him the inheritance of a holy life, which is a treasure that will not perish.' He said to his son, 'Gold and silver and jewels are not in my possession. But if you are willing to receive spiritual treasures and are strong enough to carry them and to keep them, I shall give you the Four Truths which will teach you the Eightfold Path of Righteousness. Do you desire to be admitted to the brotherhood of those who devote their life to the culture of the mind seeking the highest bliss attainable?'

Rahula replied firmly, 'I do.'

Suddhodana was naturally upset. Ananda, Gautama's cousin, had already left him for the brotherhood, and now, in addition, Rahula and his nephew Devadatta were also taken away. He spoke of his sorrow to Gautama, who agreed in future no child would be allowed to enter the Order without consent of parents or guardians.

Although Gautama permitted women to enter the Order of Nuns, and although he was inspired by Kisa Gotami before leaving on his search for truth and owed his life to the shepherd girl who gave him milk when he was dying of starvation, nevertheless, when asked by his disciples what attitude they should have towards women, he said, 'Guard against looking at a woman. If you see a woman, let it be as though you saw her not, and have no conversation with her. If after all, you must speak with her, let it be with a pure heart, and think to yourself, "I as a disciple will live in this sinful world as the

The minor goddess Sirima. A stone railing pillar from the burial mound at Bharhut, India. First century B.C.

41

Left
As in other religions, Buddhists regard
a pilgrimage as an act of faith and many
of them spend their life's savings on
going on a long pilgrimage. This man,
having reached the last years of his life,
is visiting the holy places of Nepal in
fulfilment of a vow made in his younger
days.
Right
A pilgrim from Central Asia turns a row
of prayer wheels while circumambulating
the Great Stupa at Svayambhunath,
Nepal.

Above
Buddha's footprint is carved with symbols of the 'Three Jewels' (the Buddha, the Law, and the Monkhood), the Wheel of the Law, and the Swastika.

Left
Avalokiteshvara, in the form of Padmapani, holding a lotus in his left hand. In his headdress he carries a figure of Amitabha.

Right
The White Tara ('The Tara with the Seven Eyes'). Nepalese, eighteenth century. In Tibetan Buddhism, Taras are deities in their own right, with the rank of Bodhisattva.

At this shrine in Bodh Gaya, the footprints of the Lord Buddha are worshipped with flowers with as much veneration as an image. This follows an early tradition forbidding representations of Sakyamuni which lasted until the first two centuries of the Christian Era.

46

spotless leaf of the lotus, unsoiled by the mud in which it grows.''

'If the woman be old regard her as your mother; if she be young, as your sister; if very young, as your child.'

In spite of Gautama's concern regarding the dangers of women, he was quite prepared to preach to them, whether courtesans or queens. One famous courtesan, Ambapali, hearing that the Buddha was resting in her mango grove, came to see him. She dressed herself simply and wore no ornaments, but she was beautiful in her simplicity. Gautama was impressed with her approach, for she was a favourite of princes and kings. In his experience women were filled with vanity rather than wisdom. At the end of their meeting she was full of joy at his teaching and asked if the Buddha and his followers would eat with her on the following day, to which he consented. As she was leaving the grove, the local rulers, the Licchavi Princes, arrived in magnificent carriages, gorgeously dressed in silks and wearing costly jewels. They asked Ambapali what she was doing in the grove, and she replied that she had been listening to the Blessed One and had invited him for the next day's meal. They tried to persuade her to sell them the privilege for a large sum, but she refused to give up so great an honour even if they had given her the entire territory. The Princes then tried to woo Buddha from his promise, but without effect, and returned to their palace in disgust at having been outdone, as they thought, by a frivolous girl.

The next day, after Buddha and his disciples had eaten, Ambapali gave them her house and mango grove. Many retreats were thus received by the Order, which was now growing rapidly.

Soon the wisdom of the great teacher spread beyond the border of north-east India to Burma, where the following incident is recounted in the Burmese life of the Buddha. Two princes were about to engage in a terrible battle in a quarrel over a water dyke. Between the kings and their armies Buddha suddenly appeared and asked the cause of the strife. When he was informed he said:

'Tell me, O kings. Is earth of any intrinsic value?'

Below
An elderly cymbals-player gravely takes part in the music during Buddhist worship in Bodnath Temple, Kathmandu, Nepal.
Below right
Monk musicians taking part in a Buddhist service in a temple at Svayambhunath, Nepal.

'Of no value whatever,' was the reply.

'Is water of any intrinsic value?'

'Of no value whatever.'

'And the blood of kings, is that of any intrinsic value?'

'Its value is priceless.'*

'Is it reasonable,' asked the Buddha, 'that that which is priceless should be staked against that which has no value whatever?' The angry monarchs saw the wisdom of this reasoning and abandoned their dispute.

His ministry continued for forty-five years whilst the Order expanded and the teaching became widely accepted. In his eightieth year Gautama realized that he was reaching the closing stages of his life and told his disciples to prepare for his death.

Ananda, his cousin, begged Gautama to remain with them out of pity for the world and for the good of mankind, but Buddha reminded him that it was the nature of things to die. Just as a worn-out cart can only with much difficulty be made to move, so his body could only be kept going with much additional care.

Realizing that Gautama's end was indeed near, Ananda asked him to lay down instructions for the Order before he passed away. But Buddha declined and exhorted Ananda and his followers: 'Be ye lamps unto yourselves, rely upon yourselves only and do not rely on any external help. Hold fast to the Truth as a lamp, seek salvation in the Truth, look not for assistance to anyone besides yourselves.' Gautama used the term salvation in its literal sense, that is salvation from the suffering that besets humanity in its journey through life, and not in the popular modern concept of saving an immortal soul. (The medical profession also talk of sleep being 'the salvation of the nervous system'.)

Gautama now went with his followers to Pava, and here he stayed in the mango grove of Chunda, a blacksmith. Chunda invited them to dine and prepared a special meal. When the Buddha had eaten he became ill and suffered great pain, but he bore his suffering without

* Bigandet, *Life and Legend of Gautama*, p. 191.

Left
The steps of a temple in Khatmandu, Nepal, become an extension of their home for two housewives, one of whom has hung up her washing to dry while the other feeds her baby.
Below
Statue of a monkey, possibly the monkey-god Hanuman; Patan, Nepal.

Above
A monkey steals food offerings from a shrine in Svayambhunath Temple, Kathmandu, Nepal.

Below
An elaborately carved stone door-guardian outside a temple at Bhatgaon, Nepal.

complaint and set out for Kushinara. After crossing the River Hirannavati, they reached the grove of sal trees belonging to the Mallas of Kushinara, and there he lay down on a bed that Ananda prepared for him. The Buddha rested on his right side and sent Ananda to tell the Mallas that he would pass away at the third watch in the night, and to invite them to come and see him for the last time. The Mallas came in such numbers that they could not be presented individually but were announced by families.

The Gautama addressed them for the last time, saying, 'Decay is inherent in all component things, but the Truth will remain forever! Work out your salvation with diligence.' Then he fell into deep meditation, and having passed through several stages of consciousness entered Nirvana.

The brethren who were not yet free from passions were torn with grief, but one of his followers, the venerable Anuruddha, exorted them and said: 'Enough, my brethren! Weep not, neither lament! Has not the Blessed One told us that everything that is born contains within itself the inherent necessity of dissolution. How then can it be possible that his body too should not be dissolved? Those who are free from passion will bear the loss calmly and with self-possession, mindful of the truth he has taught us.'

Then the Mallas of Kushinara gave orders to their attendants saying, 'Gather together perfume and garlands and all the music in Kushinara.' And they took the perfume and garlands and all the musical instruments to the grove where the Blessed One lay, and then, with hymns and music, paid homage to his remains.

When the funeral pyre was lit the scriptures tell that the sun and moon withdrew their shining, the earth quaked, and the sturdy forests shook like aspen leaves, whilst flowers fell untimely to the ground, so that all Kushinara became strewn knee-deep with mandara flowers. Finally, when the burning ceremonies were over, Devaputra, his chief disciple, said to the multitudes that were assembled round the pyre:

'Behold, O brethren, the earthly remains of the Blessed One have been dissolved, but the Truth which he has taught us lives in our minds and cleanses us from all sin. Let us then go out into the world, as compassionate and as merciful as our great master, and preach to all living beings the four noble Truths and the Eightfold Path of Righteousness, so that all mankind may attain to a final salvation, taking refuge in the Buddha, the Teaching and the Order.'

So ended the life of this extraordinary man, Siddhartha Gautama, the Enlightened One.

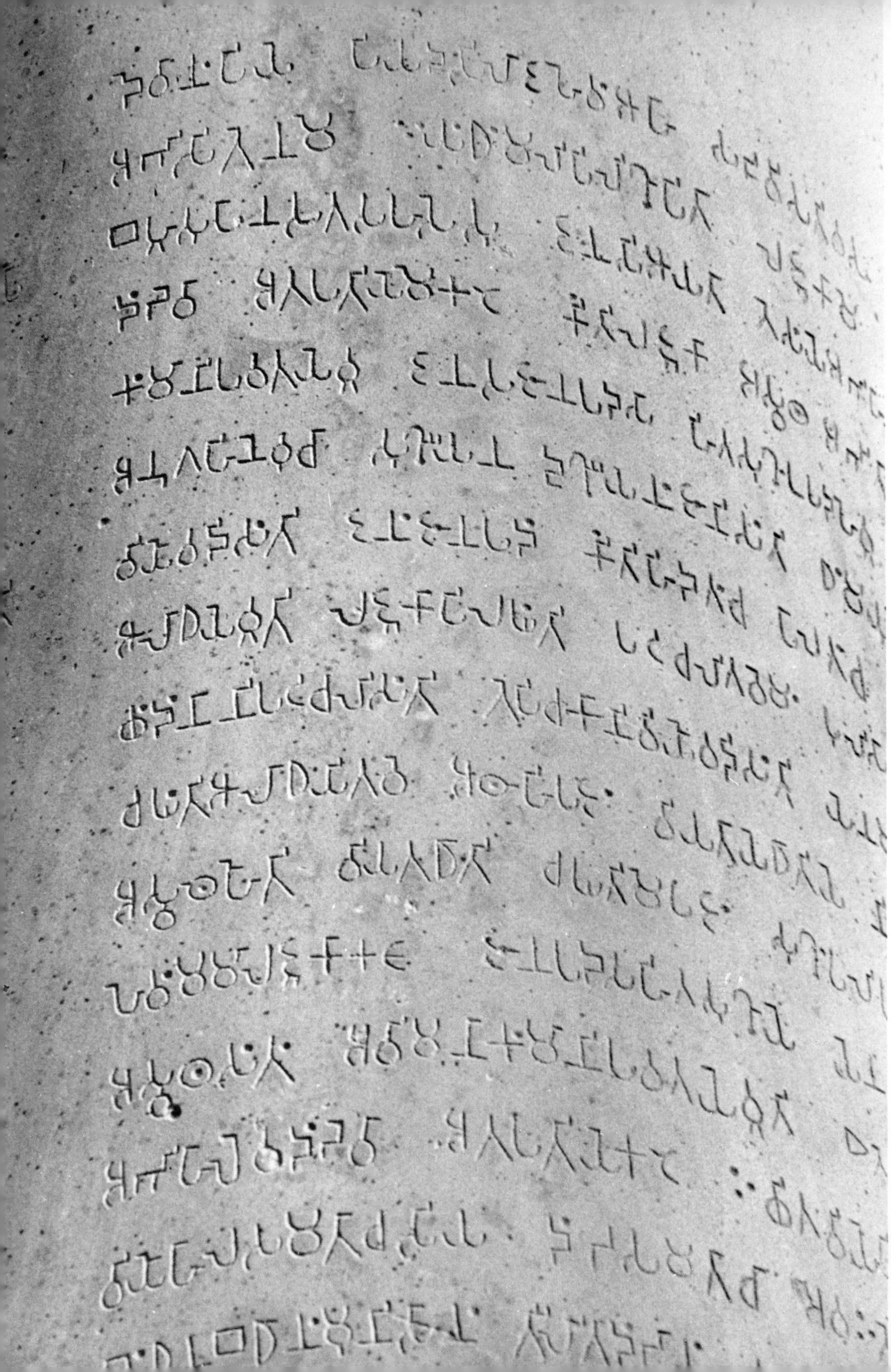

AFTER HIS DEATH

After his death (*c.* 483 B.C.) the restraining influence of Gautama's presence no longer controlled his disciples and a complicated theology sprang into growth. As the years passed, some of his followers began to consider him to be a god and, moreover, one of a whole series of divine spirits, the Buddhas. There had been many Buddhas in the past and more were to come in the future. The complications inherent in the Hindu religion gradually filtered into his teaching and under its influence theories grew and flourished. Each new supposition demanded another, until some of the original message was smothered by a mass of metaphysical subtleties. Eventually this weakened Buddhism in the very country in which it had started, but meanwhile it flourished and grew wealthy. The little groups of thatched huts were replaced by large monastic buildings; and in the third century B.C. Buddhist art began to make its appearance.

The earliest Buddhist art was influenced by Greece. Alexander the Great reached India in 326 B.C., crossing the Hindu Kush range near the kingdom of Gandhara in the north-west frontier near Peshawar. This was the meeting-place of the Hellenic and Indian worlds, and the Greek artists who came to Gandhara brought their own skills and, together with Indian craftsmen, created a style which was a blend of both. The Greeks also brought figures of the ancient gods of Egypt from Alexandria, Horus, Isis and Serapis being the most popular.

Isis became Hariti, a wicked goddess whom Buddha was supposed to have converted to goodness, and when Buddhism moved to China she became the Chinese deity, Kuan-Yin. In Japan she became Kwannon. She is beautifully portrayed in these roles, frequently holding the child-god Horus in her arms, looking very like the Virgin and Child. Votive candles were burned before these images, and offerings of models of parts of the human body in need of succour were hung before the goddess.

Alexander's invasion of India had a strong influence, not only on Buddhist art, but also on Buddhist teaching, which was considerably modified by contact with the Greek gods; the use of images as an essential element in the Buddhist cult was also mainly due to Greek example. The exchange of ideas was not all one-sided however; Buddhism was well known in Alexandria, and its influence, which flowed into the Roman empire through channels opened by Alexander, can still be traced in the Gnostic forms of Christianity.

Greek influence possibly strengthened the belief among some of the followers of Buddha that each person had an immortal soul and that this could only be saved by the intervention of the deified

Left
Detail of Ashoka's column, referred to on page 77. It carries the Pillar Edict No. VII carved in ancient Brahmi characters. This edict is concerned with reflections on the promulgation of the Dharma, Dharma as meditation and non-violence, and applications of Dharma to medical aid and welfare.
Above
Profile of the head of Buddha, carved in grey stone. From the ancient kingdom of Gandhara, west Pakistan, second to fourth century A.D.

Left
The east gateway to the ancient Khmer capital of Angkor Thom, each tower having four faces of Lokeshvara, 'the Lord who looks down'. Cambodia, late twelfth to early thirteenth century A.D.

Below left
Gods and demons pulling the body of the mythical *Naga* (Snake) flanking each side of the road leading to the Temple of Preah Khan, Cambodia, late twelfth century A.D.

Right
Statue, probably of Dharmaraja, but usually known as 'the Leper King'. From the terrace of the Leper King in the Bayon temple complex, Cambodia, late twelfth to early thirteenth century A.D.

Buddha whose help could be invoked by prayers and offerings. At no time had Gautama advocated prayer; moreover, he had rejected the possibility of an individual soul, the belief in which forced mankind into a desperate and selfish struggle for immortality. Neither had he ever regarded himself as a god. In fact it seems unlikely that he ever took the title of Buddha during his lifetime. But as we have seen, in India, unlike Alexandria, there was no written word and everything the master said had to be handed down by word of mouth and thus was easily distorted.

Alexander's triumphant march through north-west India came to a halt on the north bank of the River Beas, when his soldiers refused to go any further and he was forced to turn back, finally reaching Babylon, where he died in 323 B.C. He did not leave an heir capable of wielding his authority and his generals divided his dominions among themselves; after some years of dispute, north-west India was allocated to the founder of the Syrian monarchy, Seleukos Nikator.

While this was happening in Greece, a new power had risen in India. Chandragupta Maurya, who became the founder of the Maurya dynasty and first historical emperor of India, managed to establish a kingdom in the Valley of the Ganges which he gradually expanded, holding sway over the Indians and Greeks left by Alexander.

Thus when Seleukos, in about 303 B.C., entered India from the north-west, with the aim of governing Alexander's Indian provinces, he was confronted by Chandragupta at the head of an immense army and prudently decided to ally himself with the new power. This allowed Chandragupta to consolidate a great empire stretching across the entire plain of northern India from the western to the eastern sea.

In history there has always been a struggle for power between the priesthood and the State, and Chandragupta saw in the spreading doctrine of Buddhism an ally against the growth of the Brahmans and the rule of caste. He supported and endowed the Buddhist Order and encouraged its teaching. After a reign of twenty-four years he was succeeded by his son Bindusara, who in turn was succeeded by one of his sons named Ashokavardhana, better known as Ashoka, who came to the throne about 273 B.C. and reigned until 232 B.C.

Ashoka was one of history's great monarchs. His dominions stretched from Afghanistan to Madras and he holds the unique position of being the only military monarch on record to abandon warfare after victory. In his early years he enjoyed the life of royalty. Like Gautama before him, his days were filled with the pleasures of the chase, with dancing and music, with love-making and drinking. He was most probably a Brahmanical Hindu and a worshipper of Shiva the Destroyer. A sudden change in his beliefs was brought about by the remorse he felt for the dreadful suffering which he had inflicted on the unhappy people of Kalinga when he annexed that country in 261 B.C.

The Kalinga campaign was a turning-point in history. The suffering of the wounded and the wretchedness of the prisoners were soon

A street behind the temple of Nyatpola Deval, Bhatgaon, Nepal.

56

The Hindu temple of Nyatpola Deval ('The Temple of the Five Stages'), Bhatgaon, Nepal, built by Bhupatindra Malla, A.D. 1703. The two figures at the bottom of the steps represent wrestlers, the historic giants of the Newars, who are believed to have ten times the strength of ordinary men.

forgotten, as they have always been forgotten in the long, sad story of man's inhumanity to man; but the effect that they produced upon the conscience of the victor is still in evidence today. Ashoka himself tells us of the effect that the battle had upon him, and we are fortunate that the account has moved out of the period of hearsay and legend and is recorded in letters cut into stone, the most remarkable inscriptions in the world. Ashoka had his Edicts inscribed on granite pillars, rock caves and on boulders. Thirty-five edicts still exist, and they are the first written evidence of Buddha and his teaching. The longest is number thirteen and was written in 261 B.C. in the striking language of the period, reminiscent of that of the Pharaohs:

'Kalinga was conquered by His Sacred and Gracious Majesty when he had been consecrated eight years. One hundred and fifty thousand persons were thence carried away captive, one hundred thousand were there slain, and many times that number died. Directly after the annexation of the Kalingas began His Sacred Majesty's zealous protection of the Law of Piety, his love of that Law, and his inculcation of that Law. Thus arose His Sacred Majesty's remorse for having conquered the Kalingas because the conquest of a country previously unconquered involves the slaughter, death and carrying away captive of the people. That is a matter of profound sorrow and regret to his Sacred Majesty.'

The Edict continues that true conquest of the hearts of men can only be gained by man's acceptance of the Law and conquest of himself, the doctrine of Buddha. Ashoka devoted the rest of his life to the spreading of Buddhism throughout the world. He set up further edicts in the conquered provinces, proclaiming that all men were his children and warning his officers that they must carry out his fatherly requests in the spirit in which they were made. He grieved that some servants of the State failed to carry out his wishes and inflicted torture or unjust imprisonment on his subjects. To them he said, 'Beware of yielding to the vices of envy, lack of perseverance, harshness, impatience, want of application, laziness and indolence.'

His sons and grandsons also were told to follow the Eightfold Path of true conquest; if, he said, they unhappily became involved in conquest by force of arms, they were to be patient and gentle so that they might return to the true path and partake of the joys of the spirit.

Ashoka probably became a layman in the Buddhist community and his influence spread the gospel far beyond the boundaries of his empire. The royal preacher's work extended to the west, where the Hellenistic kings allowed him to spread the message of Buddhism in their dominions. Ashoka was a contemporary of Antiochos Theos, grandson of Seleukos Nikator, the foe and afterwards ally of his grandfather, Chandragupta; of Ptolemy Philadelphos of Egypt; of Magas, the ruler of Cyrene, and of Alexander, King of Epirus. The records confirm that his teaching throughout these distant regions

Above
Head of Lokeshvara ('the Lord who looks down') in a tower of the Bayon Temple, Cambodia, late twelfth to early thirteenth century A.D.

Right
Three-headed elephants supporting the Victory (East) Gate to the temple of Angkor Thom, Cambodia, are the mount of the Hindu god Indra. Each trunk holds a lotus blossom.

Above left
An *Apsaras* (celestial nymph), from the temple of Angkor Wat, Cambodia, late eleventh to early twelfth century A.D.
Above right
The Buddhist smile of a Laotian Girl.
Right
Benignly smiling Buddhas receive the adoration of a faithful worshipper at a shrine in a temple at Angkor, Cambodia.
Far right
After the abandonment of Angkor in the fifteenth century, it quickly fell into the grip of the jungle. French archaeologists have released and restored many of the monuments.

founded a moral code which has been handed down to the present day.

The missions of Ashoka were among the greatest civilizing influences in the history of the world. They entered countries for the most part barbarous and full of superstition. The history of Ceylon, Japan, Thailand and Tibet commenced with the advent of Buddhism. Taboos, tribal gods, evil spirits and demons gave way to the law of cause and effect, to the solid moral principles of the Eightfold Path. The Buddhist missionaries also brought with them the culture of India, irrigation, sculpture and the arts. All this is still visible and growing.

The most important mission of Ashoka's reign was to Ceylon in about 250 B.C. and was led by Mahendra, said to have been the monarch's son or younger brother. The ruler of Ceylon at that time was King Tissa, who like his friend Ashoka reigned for forty years. During his lifetime he also did all that he could to promote Buddhism, and to this day the teaching has never lost its hold upon the island. Following Mahendra came his sister, still remembered by her title, Sanghamitra, 'Friend of the Order'. She brought with her a cutting from the great Bo tree under which Gautama found enlightenment. The original tree at Bodh Gaya is dead, though another has replaced it; but the cutting still survives in the spot where it was planted in Anuradhapura, the then capital of Ceylon. The tree, a type of fig, has been carefully tended, the branches supported by pillars and earth heaped round its base so that it has always been able to put forth fresh roots. Over twenty-two centuries old, it has almost spanned the short recorded history of mankind. It has seen the endless change and ceaseless variety of human opinion, the constant rejection of old theories and acceptance of new as the human race struggles forward. Just as the tree endured in the changing world, so has the teaching of

Above left
A corner of the palace temple complex, Bangkok, showing the roofs of monasteries, and the spires of *stupas* (relic mounds) belonging to the Temple of the Emerald Buddha.
Above
Door-guardians, gaily painted and set with pieces of coloured glass and mirror, keep watch at an entrance to the Temple of the Emerald Buddha, Bangkok.

Intricate tracery of carved and painted ornament, set with coloured glass and pieces of mirror, decorates these doorways to the Temple of the Emerald Buddha, Bangkok.

Gautama, though, as frequently happens, the disciples seem to have cared more for the preservation of his tree than for his thoughts, which from the first they misunderstood and distorted.

Anuradhapura was a brilliant and enormous city, said to be large enough to house several million people; it became the Buddhist Rome and was a measure of Ashoka's influence on the world. Today its great ruins lie vast and silent, but near by, on the hill of Mahintale, the monastery founded by King Tissa for Mahendra, the Thuparama Dagoba, still stands and has been beautifully restored. Throughout the sacred ruins other dagobas rear their domes above the jungle, many of them higher than St Paul's Cathedral.

Ashoka considered spreading the Doctrine as a duty of the State, but one which was to be fulfilled by peaceful means. His inscriptions, found from the north-west frontier to Mysore, record his instructions to his missionaries to travel to the utmost limits of the barbarian countries and to intermingle with all unbelievers to spread the Doctrine. They were to mix equally with Brahmans and with beggars, with the dreaded and with the despised, teaching the Doctrine both within the kingdom and in foreign countries. Conversion was to be achieved by persuasion, never by the sword. Ashoka's central kingdom became known as the Land of the Monasteries, Bihar, and still keeps its ancient name.

Towards the end of his reign in 242 B.C., Ashoka, who had been on the throne for over thirty years, decided to review the policies taken during his reign. This review, inscribed on seven pillars, was known as the Seven Pillar Edicts (242 B.C.) and was the last event in Ashoka's life which can be accurately dated. The Fifth Pillar expressed his anxiety for the care of animals and all living creatures. He forbids the slaughter of animals and disapproves of the practice of castration. But this also pressed heavily against the Brahmanical custom of sacrifices as well as the livelihoods of hunters, fishermen and many other poor people. The discontent which must have been caused by its enforcement may have had much to do with the break-up of the empire on Ashoka's death.

Ashoka's moral code is summed up in his second Minor Rock Edict.

'Father and mother must be obeyed; similarly respect for living creatures must be enforced; Truth must be spoken. These are the virtues of the Law of Duty which must be practised.'

In the 5,000 words contained in the Edicts, Ashoka also required compassion for all living things and toleration for the creeds of others, a tolerance that finally undermined Buddhism in the country of its origin. He was a hard worker and his thoughts were reflected in his innumerable deeds for the benefit of his subjects. Hospitals, canals, wells, public parks and gardens for medicinal herbs were created. Officers were appointed for the supervision of charitable works. He created a ministry for the care of primitive subject races.

He provided for the education of women. He demonstrated the practicality of the Eightfold Path. Right thought, right effort and right livelihood marked his career.

The reign of Ashoka provided an ideal atmosphere for the development of the arts, and whilst his father and grandfather had built magnificent palaces, they had probably been built of wood and their rich ornaments made of the same perishable material. So the history of Indian art, which dates back to Mohenjo-daro about 2000 B.C., came to full flower with Ashoka, the age in which stone became widely used not only for the Edicts but also for the exquisite sculptures of the period. Because of Ashoka's missions abroad, this sculpture is influenced by Persian and Greek examples, but in spirit and execution it is mainly Indian. His craftsmen probably carved in stone as they had carved in wood, using the same techniques and designs. They worked not only the soft Indian sandstone, but also the flint-like gneiss rock, which they polished until it shone like glass.

The sculptures of the Ashokan period are so magnificent that the Indian Republic has adopted as its national seal the capital of the

Below
Wall painting from the Temple of the Emerald Buddha, Bangkok, showing an illustration from the Indian epic, *The Ramayana*, in which the monkey god Hanuman makes a bridge of his body so that Rama's army can cross from India to Ceylon.
Right
The effort of supporting a great weight is aptly expressed in the stance and twisted features of this minor god, one of a frieze supporting a stylized burial mound in the courtyard of the Temple of the Emerald Buddha, Bangkok.
Below right
Wall painting from the Temple of the Emerald Buddha, Bangkok, showing an illustration from *The Ramayana* in which the goddess of the sea is swallowing victims from the armies crossing from India to Ceylon.

Ashokan column at Sarnath, showing four lions with the Wheel of the Law, the subject of Buddha's first sermon at Sarnath. This masterpiece compares favourably with anything produced in the ancient world. The skill of Ashoka's craftsmen in carving was equalled by their engineering achievements. Their ability to handle and transport huge monolithic columns over great distances matched that of the ancient Egyptians, and just as the Egyptians depicted their daily life on the walls of their tombs, so the artists of Ashoka carved vivid pictures of the bustling cheerful life of their age. At Sanchi and Bharhut relief sculptures in stone show scenes of the period, full of charm and good taste.

The end of Ashoka's reign came shortly after the issuing of the Seven Pillar Edicts in 242 B.C., but there is no real evidence of how or where this great man passed away from the scene of his strenuous labours. For over thirty years this disciple of Buddha had worked for the real needs of mankind. Out of the tens of thousands of monarchs and majesties, eminences and serene highnesses that crowd the pages of history, the name of Ashoka is still cherished and remembered, a bright star in the dark chronicle of mankind.

Although gaily patterned with coloured glass, the fierce expression of these *Nagas* (snakes) guarding the stairway to the monastery of Doi Sutheb, North Thailand, seems to make certain that it will triumph over its traditional enemies in Indian mythology, the *garudas* (birds of prey).

A BABEL

A babel of conflicting views followed the death of Ashoka and the teaching of the Buddha became dispersed. Apart from the Edicts, no accounts were written down until some three centuries later and only one of these exists in any form of completeness. It is the Canon of the Theravadins, 'The School of the Elders', written in Pali on dried palm leaves and carefully preserved in Ceylon. This was compiled by monks from the teaching brought to the island by Mahendra and his sister, but as it was not written down until the first century A.D., the records had been preserved for three and a half centuries by memorizing and repetition so that differences from the original were inevitable. The records tell that immediately after the death of Buddha a Council of the Sangha or Order was called at Rajgir to settle the content of the Canon. A second Council was held at Vaisali about a hundred years later, and continued the attempt of the first to define what the rules of the Order should be and how the teaching should be interpreted. A third was held at Pataliputra about the time of the death of Ashoka to correct various heresies that had entered the teaching, possibly as a result of Hindu influences. The fourth and last of the great councils was held in Kashmir under the Kushan king, Kanishka. This council consisted of 500 members and compiled three commentaries on Buddhist faith which form part of the scriptures of the 'greater vehicle of the law'. This contained many corruptions of the Doctrine as originally recorded by Ashoka. All these discussions naturally led to many schisms within the Order, from which emerged two main divisions: the Hinayana, or Theravada, and the Mahayana.

The strength of the original teaching of Buddha lay in its philosophical character, which enabled the thinker – but not the masses – to understand the moral law which pervades the world. It knew no supernatural revelation and its arguments rested on probable truths. Much of this original spirit of the teaching is preserved in the School of the Elders, which is the best-known sect of the Hinayana. Hinayana is called by Buddhists 'the little vessel of salvation', for it is comparable to a small boat by which a man may cross the river of worldliness to reach the shore of Nirvana.

The Mahayana sect, whilst springing from the original Doctrine, also took nourishment from the Hindu tradition, which had always lapped on the shores of Buddhism and which pressed with ever increasing force after the death of the Leader. The tolerance of Buddhism, coupled with the need for a doctrine which would be acceptable to the masses of eager listeners, soon altered the moral philosophy for the few into salvation by faith for the many, who found

An artist at work restoring the wall paintings which line the inner compound wall of the Temple of the Emerald Buddha, Bangkok. These murals tell the story of *The Ramakien*, a romance based on the Indian epic, *The Ramayana*.

Wall painting from the Temple of the Emerald Buddha, Bangkok, showing an illustration from *The Ramayana*, in which the monkey god Hanuman defeats the King of Ceylon.

the original message too difficult to grasp. Thus the Mahayana was constructed, the large vessel of salvation in which the multitudes could find abundant room for their safe passage over the river of life.

Hinayana Buddhists looked upon Mahayana as a departure from the original teaching of Buddha, and as the Pali Hinayana texts were the basis of much of the knowledge of Buddhism brought to the West, western students have tended to share this point of view. The Mahayana believe that Buddha taught various aspects of the truth at different stages of his life, adapted to the understanding of the people he was teaching. Hinayana Buddhists also quarrelled among themselves and produced some eighteen divergent schools. From this division of beliefs it was natural for Buddhism to throw up a St Paul. His name was Asvoghosha and he was born in Oudh towards the end of the first century. Like Paul he was haughty, learned and converted – in this case to Buddhism. He attacked the caste system and took up the cause of Buddhism with tremendous vigour and enthusiasm. From this surging mind, Mahayana Buddhism grew and increased in strength as Hinduism gradually infiltrated Hinayana Buddhism.

It may be said that as Paul's theology naturally stemmed out of the teaching of Christ, so did Mahayana philosophy stem out of the teaching of Buddha. It was to be a vastly more popular interpretation of the Teaching. Dissatisfied with the doctrine of Nirvana as extinction of self, it regarded the salvation of the few, however difficult such salvation might be, as being selfish, and regarded the salvation of the many through the doctrine of Bodhisattvas as being of greater merit.

The new doctrine did not contradict the old, but taught that each individual should aim at attaining Enlightenment for himself so that he might preach to others and serve the welfare of all. One who made this his goal became a Bodhisattva and set out on a course of training by which, through many rebirths, he acquired great merit. The aim of this training was not to transform all disciples into saviours but to make the ordinary man look for salvation to the Bodhisattvas, who by their virtue could save beings from hell and assure rebirth in heaven to all those who devoutly repeated their names. Bodhisattvas voluntarily returned to earth, postponing their Buddhahood in order that the world might be saved, and not until all mankind were saved could they rest in peace.

The new doctrine also supported prayer and devotion and salvation by faith rather than by works – meditation was always a strong point with the Indian mind and was very acceptable in other countries. Finally it made Buddha into a god. Such a development could hardly have been prevented; it followed naturally from man's instinct to worship. Veneration of dictators and leaders in every field from pop singers to philosophers has always been part of human make-up, and although Buddhism was soon to recede in its country of origin, the tide of faith was flowing in ever-increasing strength to other countries.

It is interesting to realize that, apart from Buddhism, India gave

Left
Although much remains to be learnt about the civilization of Central Asia, we know that it was once a stronghold of Buddhism. This wall painting of a cowherd comes from Qizil and was made about the year A.D. 500.

Right
Tibetan Buddhism has been profoundly influenced by Indian Tantric texts. This accounts for the appearance of the tutelary deity Shamvara, seen with his partner Vajravarahi in this eighteenth century Tibetan painting.

the world, philosophy, the study of grammar, phonetics, chess, algebra, produced the story of the Arabian nights and inspired such writers as Goethe, Schopenhauer, Boccaccio and Aesop. India is a land intoxicated by religion, and herein lies its strength and also its weakness, for there is not one god but many. The total runs into millions, and out of this multitude it is possible to find support for almost any mode of life. There are cults and deities for all and salvation for all. Buddha, on the other hand, accepts man's mentality, his personality and his spiritual constitution, but he denies the existence of any mysterious ego-entity which by some schools was supposed to reside behind or within man's bodily and physical activities as a distinct being, a separate thing in itself, a metaphysical agent. Buddha claimed that a man's self is made up of thoughts alone. The thoughts of a man constitute his self and there is no additional or separate 'self' besides. No man's thoughts remain still, and so the self of man changes continually from moment to moment: salvation, Buddha said, lies in a man's own hands and must be sought for by him. The principal difference is between the emphasis which Buddha lay on working out one's own salvation with diligence and the Mayahana which taught that salvation could be obtained by prayer to the Bodhisattvas and to Buddha.

The idea of a 'separate self' behind the man is common not only to India, but to the rest of the world, a tribute to man's habitual egotism. Buddha regarded this as an illusion growing out of the vanity of worldliness, inducing man to believe that the purpose of his life lies in his self. Buddha proposed to cut off all thought of self, so that it could no longer bear fruit. Thus Buddha's Nirvana is a state of mind in which the man is no longer concerned with personal selfishness and so becomes a habitation for truth. The essence of man consists of his karma – the distillation of his innumerable lives, from the dark jungles where his predecessors fought with blood-red dripping fangs to the sophisticated society of today. It is the fruit of all the seed he has sown and all the harvests he has reaped. It is the inevitable reaction that follows his every action. It is that part of the human race which continues its long journey through births and deaths until finally it lets go of the darkness of the past and emerges into the happiness of an unselfish future.

Thus, by denying the existence of that which appears to be our soul, and for the judgement of which in death we tremble, Buddha actually, as he himself says, opens the door of salvation to mankind: 'He who loses his soul shall save it.' This is the cornerstone of his teaching and the comfort which is so enthusiastically received by his followers. Anyone who fails to appreciate the positive aspect of Buddhism will be unable to understand how it can exercise such a powerful influence upon millions and millions of people.

The religious zeal which gave rise to Mahayana Buddhism cannot be denounced any more than Christianity can be criticized on account of its dogmatology and mythological ingredients. Christianity has succeeded in giving a religion of charity and mercy to the most powerful nations in the world. It extends its message of universal goodwill with the least amount of restriction to the natural selfishness that is so strongly developed in the Western races. Christianity is the religion of love made easy, and is even more adapted to the needs of the multitudes than the large vessel of Mahayana.

Many parallels have been shown between Christianity and Buddhism and the central core of each was expressed by Christ's 'Know thyself'. Centuries later Shakespeare wrote, 'This above all – To thine own self be true; and it must follow, as the night the day, thou can'st not then be false to any man.' For above all religions is the Religion of Truth.

Left
A Buddhist monk, with shaven head and wearing an orange robe, sits in the bright sunlight of a doorway in Doi Sutheb at Chieng Mai, North Thailand.
Right
Mythical figures disport themselves amongst foliage. A design in mother-of-pearl on black lacquer on a temple door in Bangkok.

Zenkei Shibayama
Kancho (Chief Priest) of the
Zen monastery in Kyoto.
Over half a century as a Zen
scholar and teacher has left
him full of vitality yet with
a warm sense of humour
and a serenity which comes
from a profound inner
sense of peace.

The head of the colossal figure of Buddha at Kamakura, Japan. This bronze statue was erected in A.D. 1252 and weighs 210,000 pounds. The Buddha is seated in the posture of meditation.

THE DECLINE

The truth of Buddhism in India declined as the veneration for the dead Teacher passed into the worship of a living Saviour. The seeds of decay were sown at the same time as the conversion of Ashoka caused that great king to send the doctrine of Gautama from the banks of the Ganges to the snows of the Himalayas, the deserts of Central Asia and the bazaars of Alexandria. The teaching, so well suited to the people of India, required fundamental changes before it could move hearts of its new listeners. During the unification of the civilized world under the rule of the Caesars, nascent Christianity met mature Buddhism in the markets and academies of Asia and Egypt. Here both teachings were exposed to the influences of paganism in many forms and countless works of art which favoured polytheism. In this environment it was inevitable that the ferment of human thought and the clash of rival civilizations would produce change.

The rigorous doctrine of the earliest form of Buddhism was too chilly to retain a hold upon the hearts of men unless warmed by human emotion. Buddhism adopted by people in other countries has always differed from the original teaching, although still retaining much common ground. But whatever interpretation may be given to the Doctrine, one result is abundantly clear: it produced works of art that compare favourably with any so far created by the hand of man. Some of the finest art in India, Ceylon, Burma and Thailand is Buddhist, and the greatest art of Tibet, Nepal, China and Japan followed the introduction of Buddhism.

At first the Buddha was considered to be too sacred to be shown in person, and in consequence was represented by his footprints, an empty saddle or throne, the Bodhi Tree, a stupa, or the Wheel of the Law. Not until some four centuries after his death is Gautama depicted as the deified Buddha. Of the earliest art, nothing survives as everything was executed in perishable wood. With the reign of Ashoka, Indian craftsmen took to the use of stone, but so accustomed were they to the sacred quality of the wooden figures that the stone equivalents were carved like wood and retained the joints and surfaces one would find in carpentry.

Gradually the simplicity of the earlier forms changed into carvings and paintings filled with sensuous delight, breathing erotic attraction, like the Ajanta Frescoes, the temples of Ellora and others which spread through the vast sub-continent. Many of the more important works have been placed in museums or brought to the principal cities. Firuz Shah, 1351–88, brought one of Ashoka's pillars to the new city

Two female figures painted on a rock face at Sigirya, Ceylon. Fifth century A.D.

of Delhi, which he was building and which he named after himself, Firuzabad. The inscription on the tall white pillar is as sharp and clear as if it had been freshly carved. The transport of this huge monolith required a special carriage with forty-two wheels, and it is said that to each wheel was attached a rope upon which 200 men pulled, making a total labour force of 8,400. This acquisition of Indian art was not confined to Firuz Shah. From all parts of the civilized world came demands for the sculpture and painting of India; some was paid for, some plundered. Today every important museum in the world contains examples of Buddhist art, but they look forlorn in their austere surroundings, which naturally enough lack the warm sensuous atmosphere of the sunlit temples of their original setting. No one who has made the journey to the rock-hewn caves of Ajanta and Ellora, the shrines of Bodh Gaya and Sarnath or any of the well-known sites, can fail to be impressed by the centuries-old saturation of religious feeling which pervades everything, the air one breathes, the stones one treads. It lingers in the quiet movement of the scented leaves and in the shimmering haze of heat beyond their shadow. India, beyond all doubt, is a land intoxicated with religion.

The great river of exotic art that flowed over India in the Gupta period (A.D. 320–647) is difficult to relate to the simple teachings of Buddha. The Buddhists, however, distinguish between the appreciation of the abstract beauty of Enlightenment and its perishable forms. The Buddha himself renounced the world and all its vanities, but the order he founded used the artistic abilities of Indian craftsmen to enhance its propaganda. The snares of desire they proclaim attract the multitude of ordinary people, who in time may learn from the cool indifference of the Buddha to reject such worldliness. In the Pali Canon there is a conversation between Buddha and his cousin and favourite disciple Ananda. Ananda asks about the holy life, wondering whether it should be half composed of friendship, intimacy and association with all that is beautiful. Buddha leaves him in no doubt; he replies that this is the whole, not half, of the holy life of those who tread the Eightfold Path. But the association is pure love and appreciation of beauty without jealous envy of desire and possession. There is nothing gloomy about Buddhism, nothing pessimistic. A man who is free from the desire of possession is free to enjoy all the delights of the senses and the beauty of life.

After the seventh century in India, Buddhism began to wane. It was too open, too tolerant, too lacking in the dark mysterious labyrinths of sensuous allure that Hinduism conjured up to survive in the land of its origin. It admitted no caste, no race superiority, it submitted to no earthly and still less to any heavenly authority. 'Work out your own salvation,' said he who had done so. 'The house of self is on fire and the wise man concentrates on leaving it.' Blind faith has no part in Buddhism. Buddha himself only pointed to a way of living, his followers can only test the truth of his teaching by trying it for themselves.

Left
It is often said that Buddhism is a pessimistic religion. Buddhists themselves, however, are no more pessimistic than followers of any other religion. It would not be far wrong to say that this happy, smiling Tibetan girl expresses the character of most Buddhists.

Right
The White Tara is the goddess of perfect purity leading to transcendent wisdom which bestows everlasting bliss. With her right hand she bestows charity, and with her left she controverts the arguments against Buddhism.

The Muslim conquest finally ended the gentle hold of Buddhism in its last area in India, Bihar. In 1193 Sultan Muhammad Ghuri captured Bihar and, indifferent to the distinction between Brahmans, Jains and Buddhists, put all the 'shaven-headed idolaters' to the sword. Some were fortunate enough to escape the massacre and fled to Nepal and Tibet, but after A.D. 1200 almost all traces of Buddhism in upper India had disappeared. Even Bodh Gaya, the sacred place of the Enlightenment, was transformed into a temple dedicated to Vishnu and Shiva, with Buddha relegated to a place among the ten manifestations of Vishnu. Thus Buddhism in India, after a vigorous life lasting more than 1,000 years, declined and almost came to an end. So too did the Bodhi Tree, in the cycle of nature which demands that all things pass away in their allotted time, but from its roots sprang a shoot which flourishes there today, and as the parent plant withered its seeds were carried around the world and rooted strongly in many alien soils.

Below left
Coppergilt figure of a Buddhist sage next to the entrance of a small shrine, Patan, Nepal.
Below right
A mythical beast (*Kinnara*), half-human, half-bird, helps to protect the compound of the Temple of the Emerald Buddha, Bangkok.
Right
Head of Lokeshvara, of carved and painted wood. Nepalese, eighteenth century.
Far right
Wall painting from the Temple of the Emerald Buddha, Bangkok, showing an illustration from *The Ramayana* in which Rama sets out for battle with the forces of Ceylon.

THE SEED

The seed of Buddhism first came to Ceylon, where not only did the cutting from the original Bodhi Tree in Gaya take root, but the doctrine also found fertile soil, and both still thrive today. The Theravada, or the 'Doctrine of the Elders' as it is known, is still a living force, and it was from this island that its message spread to the rest of the world.

It flowered in many lands and the flowers were beautiful and varied; not only in Ceylon, but also in Tibet, Burma, Nepal, Thailand, Cambodia, Vietnam, Laos, Indonesia, China and Japan. The rich creative cultures of these countries were encouraged by the Teaching that brought comfort to all mankind. One of the strongest Buddhist convictions is that it is not possible to express in words what is most real, sublime and ultimate. For this reason even the finest, most lucid and consistent doctrine can only be regarded as provisional and as obscuring the ultimate truth rather than revealing it.

Above
Perhaps hardship and misfortune have left their mark on the face of this Chinese woman. Now, with deep devotion, she lights a joss-stick before her favourite image to seek his help.

Right
It is through his compassion that a Bodhisattva postpones his entry into Nirvana in order to help other mortals to escape rebirth. The sculptor of this Chinese figure has convincingly realized in stone the essential compassion of a Bodhisattva.

Far left
By its combination of facial expression and hand gesture, this Tibetan bronze figure of the Bodhisattva Sarvanivaranavishkambhin subtly conveys the spirit of compassion which is one of the ultimate ideals of all Bodhisattvas.
Left
Vishnu riding on a Garuda, Javanese, eleventh century.
Below left
This bronze shows male and female deities in a loving embrace which is explained by Tibetan lamas as the penetration of the physical state by the spiritual force.

Unlimited tolerance is an essential element of Buddhism; hence it could adapt itself to alien ways of thinking without sacrificing its basic consepts. It never considered dominating the lives and thoughts of the people under its sway as other religions have endeavoured to do. It had no concept of a Jealous God. In India this led to its almost complete reabsorption into Hinduism, but in China it absorbed the Confucianist and Taoist elements and in Japan Shintoism. Buddhism not only adapted itself to other spiritual influences, it also transformed them and stimulated their development towards its own qualities of compassion. In India the Brahmans, after winning their long fight with Buddhism, never quite returned to the bloody sacrifices and intolerance of the past.

Tibet

Overleaf, left
A rather primitive sculptural style emphasizes the fierceness of this painted image of Bhairava. It is in the main square of the city of Kathmandu, Nepal.
Overleaf, right
The laughing monk Hotei in the Tiger Balm Garden, Singapore.

The Tibetans live in a country of vast empty, silent spaces, cut off from the rest of the world by colossal mountains. The average height of the land above sea-level is some 16,000 feet and the rarified atmosphere and loneliness of the small communities proved fertile ground for magic and sorcery. Buddhism was introduced into the country in the seventh century when the powerful ruler, King Song-tsen Gampo, married a princess from China and another from Nepal. Both were Buddhists and between them they converted the king. Song-tsen Gampo commenced to preach and to build temples and became the founder of Tibetan Buddhism. With its usual tolerance, the new religion accepted much of the ritual that was already prevalent in the magic rites performed by the Shaman or sorcerer, who was the dominant figure in the Bon, a form of nature worship then practised not only in Tibet but also from Central Asia to eastern Siberia. In the great Potola monastery at Lhasa, before the recent Chinese invasion, the Dalai Lama was enthroned as the 'living Buddha'. Here hundreds of priests, abbots and lamas carried out services of great beauty before a golden figure of Buddha on the high altar. The service was conducted by priests in vestments accompanied by the ringing of bells and the chanting of sacred prayers, reverently heard by the congregation in an atmosphere scented with incense. Throughout the land prayer wheels turned, holding the attention of the senses whilst the mind concentrated on meditation. Long silken banners bearing the magic words '*Om mani padme hum*', 'The jewel is in the

lotus', hung from many flagpoles. Whenever the flag moved it breathed a prayer for its owner. A modern translation might read:

Om – possessing wisdom
ma – Buddha
ni – whose tranquil nature removes evil
pad – and spreads the qualities of goodness
me – his power brings people to possess these qualities
hum – by his strength he overcomes evil.

Tibetan Buddhism contains some of the purest Buddhist principles. From this teeming world of monks and nuns, from the great monastery of De-pung, which holds 10,000 men, to the tiny settlements in the remote hills, many objects of great beauty and terrifying aspect have sprung. The famous paintings of the demon of self clinging to the Wheel of Life show the twelve states of man in the chain of causation:

1 Blind unknowing existence.
2 Desires form.
3 Feelings emerge.
4 Individuals arise from feelings.
5 Individuals develop five senses and a mind.
6 The five senses and the mind come into contact with things.
7 Contact causes sensation.
8 Sensation creates craving.
9 Craving clings to things.
10 Clinging increases selfhood.
11 Selfhood continues in renewed births.
12 Renewed births are the cause of suffering and death, and in turn lead back to Cause 1 and a new beginning to the cycle.

They deal with the physical relationship between the different states of feeling, emotion, action, and circumstances which affect all living beings alike. In the centre, surrounded by heaven and hell, are a cock, a pig and a snake, representing lust, sloth and hatred. These three passions form the basic desires of selfish and wordly existence. Everyone who lives in the world is subject to them. The letting go of the wheel of life is the attainment of Nirvana. Dr Paul Carus has expressed this in his excellent book *The Gospel of Buddha* as follows:

'In the beginning there is existence blind and without knowledge, and in this area of ignorance there are appetences formative and organizing. From appetences, formative and organizing rises awareness or feelings. Feelings beget organisms that live as individual beings. These organisms develop six fields, that is, the five senses and the mind. The six fields come in contact with things. Contact begets sensation. Sensation creates the thirst of individualized being. The thirst of being creates a cleaving to things. The cleaving produces the growth and continuation of selfhood. Selfhood continues in renewed births. The renewed births of selfhood are the cause of suffering, old age, sickness and death. They produce lamentation, anxiety and despair.

Left
A statue of the Hindu god Vishnu riding on his mount Garuda. Java, probably tenth century A.D.

Below left
A worshipper before the figure of Shakyamuni seated in the 'Earth Witness' position; Siamese Buddhist 'Temple of a Thousand Lights', Singapore.

Below
A worshipper at the reclining figure of the Buddha Shakyamuni passing into Nirvana; scene in the Siamese Buddhist temple, the 'Temple of a Thousand Lights', Singapore.

'The cause of all sorrow lies at the very beginning; it is hidden in the ignorance from which life grows. Remove ignorance and you will destroy the wrong appetences that rise from ignorance; destroy these appetences and you will wipe out the wrong perception that rises from them. Destroy wrong perception and there is an end of errors in individualized beings. Destroy errors in individualized beings and the illusion of the six fields will disappear. Destroy illusions and the contact with things will cease to beget misconception. Destroy misconception and you do away with thirst. Destroy thirst and you will be free of all morbid cleaving. Remove the cleaving and you destroy the selfishness of selfhood. If the selfishness of selfhood is destroyed you will be above birth, old age, disease and death and you escape all suffering.'*

* Paul Carus, *The Gospel of Buddha*, p. 31.

Overleaf, left
In this low relief stone sculpture from Gandhara, the Buddha is seated on a lotus preaching to many gods and goddesses. It may illustrate the second of the two great miracles at Sravasti in which, after two Naga kings had created a lotus for the Buddha to sit upon, he multiplied other lotuses with Buddhas on them all around him.

Overleaf, right
Mi-lo-fo, 'The Laughing Buddha', in the Siong Lim See Temple, Singapore, is a form of Maitreya, the Buddha to be. He is a popular deity in South-East Asia and some parts of China. His rounded cheerfulness also makes him attractive to westerners, who often mistake him for the Buddha.

Buddhism in Tibet, no less than in its other forms, partakes of the complex collection of gods, minor gods, saints and spiritual beings which have become grafted onto the original teaching. Here the hierarchy descends from the Adi-Buddha, who is the one eternal living principle of the entire Universe. He works through five Buddhas. These five, unlike Gautama, were Buddhas from the beginning and had never been anything else. During the period of evolution they produce a number of Bodhisattvas of varying degrees of advancement. One of these manifests himself in human form and becomes known to mankind as the Buddha. Thus the spiritual advance of the world is a carefully calculated operation, with constant guidance from the Absolute to the human leaders of mankind. The next human Buddha, who will come to earth in some hundreds of thousands of years, is Maitreya, and he is constantly worshipped together with Avalokiteshvara, literally 'the Lord who is seen', the Omnipresent Universal Spirit 'of nature'. He is the Padmapani, the Lotus-born and the being to whom the prayer of Tibet, '*Om mani padme hum*', is continually poured out.

The multiplicity of gods and godlings provided for worship is explained by various lamas, who say that the minds of men are given to superstition and it is better that they should find their superstitions prepared for them with a definite object in view rather than let them invent their own. The deeper teachings are beyond the capacity of the majority, and if superstition helps the people to a better way of life, why remove it? Superstition is found in the thoughts of mankind

Below left
Miniature *stupas*, of stone carved with
figures of the Buddhas of the four directions,
in a sunlit corner of a square in Kathmandu,
Nepal.

Above left
Nepal is famous for its wood-carvers. They
make many icons, not only Buddhist but also
Hindu. In addition they carve intricate
architectural details, such as this window.

Right
Doorway of a temple in Kathmandu, Nepal,
carved with figures of mythological
monsters: top, a *kirtimukha* (half-animal,
half-man), and *makaras* (half-fish, half-
reptile).

Left
A monk looks across the swirling waters of the river Chao Phya towards Wat Arun (Temple of the Dawn), Bangkok, with its towers silhouetted against the setting sun.
Right
The Lord Buddha was helped in his work by two disciples, Maudgalyayana and Shariputra, the second of whom is seen here as he appears in the Phor Kark See Temple, Singapore.

all over the world. The conscious and subconscious minds are filled with beliefs that stretch far back into the history of our beginnings. Man has always been afflicted with dreads and fears common to his environments. The results of these forebodings are nowadays treated in the West by psychiatrists. But notwithstanding the efficacy of drugs, operations, shock therapy and psychoanalysis, the mental hospitals are always full. Mental stability is more common in the East, which has always shown a greater interest in the deeper meaning of life. All spirituality has had to be periodically renewed by an influx from the East. Take away the Oriental elements in Greek philosophy, take away Moses, Jesus Christ, Saint Paul and Mahomet, and there would have been no spiritual thought in the West during the past 2,000 years. In the East all men bring their spiritual bowls to the table of life and whatever the size or shape each is filled to overflowing.

To the Western mind the idea of magic has been replaced by science, but even in the West no religion has become mature without embracing both the spiritual and the magical. If it rejects the spiritual it becomes a force without compassion dominating mankind, including those who brought it into being. If it rejects magic, the miracles of the Bible, the Grotto of Lourdes, the Transubstantiation, then it cuts itself off from the living forces of the world to such an extent that it cannot bring the spiritual side of man to maturity. The magic of

Tibetan Buddhism is regarded in the same way as the vessels of the Hinayana and Mayana – as a raft to support the weak in crossing the river of becoming. The multitude of deities, both beautiful and terrible, or the coupled figures of the Yab-yum, representing the penetration of the material by the spiritual, are no more than the symbols of higher forces and not to be worshipped, still less appeased. The spiritual power in Tibet is held by the Dalai Lama, who has now been driven into exile in India by the Chinese. His spiritual empire covers millions of Buddhists in the vast spaces of outer Mongolia and it remains to be seen whether the new materialism of the Chinese will engulf the minds and aspirations of these people.

Nepal

To the south of Tibet lies the small kingdom of Nepal, some 54,000 square miles in area. Here Gautama was born, a fact which was confirmed by the finding in 1896 of two pillars recording the visit of Ashoka. Two years later W. Peppe found in the same area a stone vase containing fragments of bone and other relics bearing the inscription: 'Receptacle of the relics of Buddha, the holy one'.

The peoples of Nepal are mostly Buddhists and, as in Tibet, regard the Dalai Lama as a god and the supreme head of their religion. They are a tough, wiry hill people and among the best known of the Oriental races despite the remoteness of their country. It is in Nepal that the famous Sherpas live on the high land below Mount Everest and the other great peaks. They are devout Buddhists and regard the huge mountains as deities. Mount Everest, 29,028 feet, is Chomolunga, 'Goddess Mother of the World', Makula, 27,824 feet, 'Goddess of Destruction'. Tenzing Norgay reached the summit of Everest with Sir Edmund Hillary in 1953 and Nawang Combu with James W. Whittaker in 1963 and again in 1965 on the Indian expedition. Only those who have climbed in these regions know the human qualities which are necessary to survive in such impossible conditions. Without the unswerving loyalty and unselfishness of the Sherpa porters no human foot would ever have trodden the summit of Mount Everest.

Throughout Nepal prayer wheels turn endlessly, some by water, some by wind and the remainder by innumerable hands. On all sides rocks and boulders bear the inscription 'Om mani padme hum', whilst overhead prayer flags flutter in the breeze. Superstition may

Far left
Doorway to the Temple of Banteay Srei, showing guardian lions and elaborately carved pediments. Cambodia, second half of tenth century A.D.
Left
A brass Tibetan holy-water vessel in the form of a head of a guardian of the faith.
Above
Heads probably forming the top of a large Tibetan bronze statue of Avalokiteshvara.

97

A monk taking a stroll round the monastery of Doi Sutheb, Chieng Mai, North Thailand.

The intricate designs which ornament the doorway in the Temple of the Emerald Buddha, Bangkok, are reminiscent of the flowing Gothic tracery of North European cathedrals.

be scoffed at, but the fact remains that these people have been able to live happy and useful lives in situations which would seem intolerable to the average Westerner.

Burma

South-east of Nepal lies Burma, where the seed fell on receptive soil and inspired the incredibly beautiful Ananda and Shwe Dagon Pagodas as well as thousands of others which proclaim the Teaching throughout the land. The earliest inhabitants came from the Mongol tribes of China and Tibet. Later arrivals came from India, and their Hindu mythology ousted Mongolian traditions, but Buddhism, subdued by Hinduism in India, reversed the situation in Burma and through its effective monastic system has directed the religious life of the people for over 1,500 years. The spiritual head of every village is the yellow-robed Buddhist monk. The monastery is also the school.

Below left
Dancing *Apsarases* (celestial nymphs), from a pillar in the Bayon Temple, Cambodia, late twelfth to early thirteenth century A.D.
Below
A bronze figure of the Buddha wearing a crown and royal attire. It was made in Burma, where such figures are called 'Jambhupati Buddhas', probably in the eighteenth century.

There are no temples as such, but pagodas crown almost every hill, silent reminders of the teaching. The result of this long association with Buddhism has been a happy people with a keen sense of humour whose women enjoy almost equal status with the men.

Thailand

Just across the Burmese frontier is Thailand. Like those of Burma the Thai monasteries throughout the country have cared for the education of the people. A very close connection exists between the people and the priesthood, for the Buddhists teach that every man should enter the order for at least two months during his lifetime, and this is usually observed.

From the great and lovely city of Bangkok to the smallest villages Buddhist temples flaunt themselves in the sunny air. Their architecture is the gayest and happiest in the world. From the eaves of the multiple-tiered roofs hang thousands of tiny bells; with clappers

A cock-fight, from a low relief sculpture on the Bayon Temple, Cambodia, late twelfth to early thirteenth century A.D.

101

A Thai soldier makes an act of worship in the Temple of Doi Sutheb, Chieng Mai, by placing a small square of gold leaf on a consecrated wall.

Kinaras, half-human half-bird, stand on the terrace of the golden *stupa* in the Temple of the Emerald Buddha, Bangkok.

Head of Brahma. Cambodia, Khmer period, eleventh or twelfth century.

made like leaves of the bodhi tree; moving in the slightest breeze they fill the air with delicate sounds. The timber roofs are covered with glazed tiles of red, blue and green arranged in intricate geometric patterns and rising in several tiers. The end of each tier is framed with long carved and inlaid roof-trees shaped like crested serpents, and the gables are encrusted with mosaics of brightly coloured glass, gilt, mirrors and pieces of porcelain which sparkle and flash in the sunlight. The origin of the snake motif, which is also found in Cambodian temples, probably goes back to Neolithic times, in which the cult of the snake was conspicuous.

The doors of the temple are as exciting as the roofs. Made from solid teak, they are thickly coated with jet-black lacquer inlaid with mother-of-pearl in exquisite designs which gleam softly iridescent in the shade. The window shutters are also richly decorated in the same way. Surrounding the courtyard in which the temple stands are a series of galleries open on the temple side but closed on the outside except for four doors opening into the courtyard. These entrances may be guarded by colossal statues of demons and the inner walls flanked with rows of images of Buddhas or covered with delicate painting of scenes from the *Ramayana*. It is a perfect example of the tolerance of Buddhism that in a totally Buddhist country scenes from Brahman theology appear everywhere. The long galleries are an adaptation from the Khmer architecture, which reaches its finest example in the great Wat at Angkor in Cambodia. The stupa or shrines in the grounds are usually set on a terraced base surrounded by Garudas, fabulous birdmen, covered with gold leaf or gilt glass.

The most famous temple is Wat Phra Keo, the Temple of the

104

Emerald Buddha in Bangkok. The Buddha is carved from a single block of translucent green jasper 24 inches high and came from Ceylon about A.D. 1400. Since its arrival it has been the most sacred object in Thailand and important state ceremonies are held before it. The Emerald Buddha has three changes of dress for the three seasons: the rainy, the cold and the hot. They are made of pure gold studded with jewels. Close by in the library is the Thai version of the Pali Canon, which was completed during the religious council held in Bangkok in 1788.

On the walls of the galleries which surround the temples are painted scenes from the *Ramayana*, the most ancient epic conceived by the men of Asia, those Aryans who are our ancestors. Long, long ago Rama, eldest son of Dasaratha, King of Ayodhya, won for himself a beautiful wife named Sita. Unfortunately, owing to jealous interference, the king was obliged to exile the lovers to a distant forest. One day, while Rama was out hunting, Sita was carried off by Ravana, a ten-headed demon, to his kingdom in Ceylon. Rama at once set out in pursuit and was assisted by Sugriva, King of the Monkeys, who lent him his monkey general Hanuman. Eventually a great bridge was built by the monkey army from India to Ceylon, known to this day as Adam's Bridge, and Ravana was overthrown. Rama and Sita returned to Ayodhya, where they became king and queen and governed wisely and lived happily for the rest of their lives.

Such, briefly, is the theme of the *Ramayana*, that legend preserved for posterity by prodigious labour of the poet Valmiki, who recorded it in a poem of 25,000 verses. The vast mural shows with infinite detail and fineness of line the magnificent march of the story. Should the legend say that a hundred warriors were slain in a certain

Below
A mythical beast, half-man, half-bird, guarding the temple of Banteay Srei, Cambodia, second half of tenth century A.D.

Below right
Part of a low-relief sculpture, showing a battle between the Cham and Khmer armies, on the outer gallery of the Bayon Temple, Cambodia, late twelfth to early thirteenth century A.D.

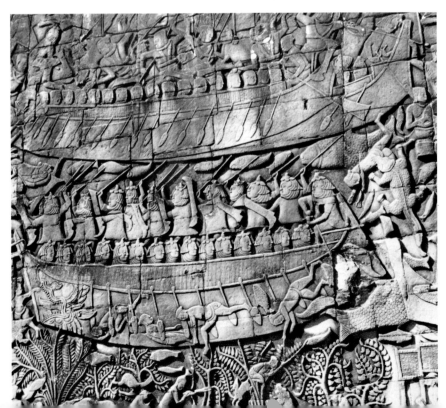

Left
The head of a *Yaksha* or demon which guards the Temple of Wat Arun, Bangkok.
Right
The golden head of a *Kinara*, half-man half-bird, in the Temple of the Emerald Buddha in Bangkok.

Left
The scene carved on this door lintel from the temple of Banteay Srei, Cambodia, is taken from a version of the Indian epic poem called the *Ramayana*.
Right
A Tibetan painting of the 'Wheel of Life'. This illustrates, in pictorial form, the fundamental beliefs of Buddhism; it can be used for the instruction of people who can neither read nor write.

Left
The complete image of this figure of the
reclining Buddha in the Wat Po, Bangkok, is
about 150 feet long and 35 feet high. Made of
plastered brick covered with gilt bronze, its
construction was an act of faith by King
Rama III of Thailand.

Right
The shrine of Svayambhunath, according to
tradition, stands on the site where Manjushri
drained the valley which became ancient
Nepal. The thirteen rings represent the
thirteen stages on the path to enlightenment.
The painted eyes are those of the all-seeing
supreme Buddha, sometimes called
Vairochana.

battle, then the whole hundred will appear lying in pools of blood and the artist will have done his best to have given each a different death stroke. Heads roll on the ground, half-severed necks sprout crimson, arrows and spears protrude with horrible reality from every part of the body, and here and there a death-ray has turned its victim bright green or blue.

In some of the paintings several perspectives have been combined to portray the scene more effectively. The wall of the palace is seen from the view-point of a beggar standing outside the gate; the palace garden as though from the top of the surrounding wall; the palace itself from the garden and the secrets of the inner courtyard from directly above. Although blood plays a large part in the story, there are charming touches. The deadly arrows of the Demon King flutter to the ground, harmless flowers, before the serene face of Rama, to remind us of the legend of Buddha and Mara's thunderbolts turning into lotus blossoms.

The Thais claim that their Order of Buddhism leads in preserving the Rules, the Burmese that theirs leads in mind development and psychology, whilst the Order in Ceylon conserves the teachings of the Buddha. Jointly this trinity proudly maintains the Theravada tradition, which to many is the nearest approach to the original teaching. These teachings all rely on the Pali Canon called the Tripitaka, or 'Three Baskets', because the three scriptures in volumes of palm leaf could just be contained in them.

Below
The Buddhist temple of Siong Lim See, Singapore.
Below right
Monks intercede on behalf of worshippers at a shrine dedicated to the ashes of their ancestors; Phor Kark See Temple, Singapore.
Right
This Tibetan ritual dagger (*phur-bu*) is used in tantrik ceremonies to exorcise evil spirits.

Cambodia

Bordering the south-east frontier of Thailand is Cambodia. This fascinating country contains many beautiful ruins of the Khmer civilization, including the famous temple of Angkor Wat. Originally built as a Hindu temple it was, like the other ancient temples of Cambodia, at times occupied by Buddhists. Like the Greeks, the Khmers did not know how to build the arch, and all the galleries and chambers of the great temple of Angkor Wat are governed in size by the length that stone rafters could conveniently be made for the ceilings. The result is dark mysterious interiors in which images of the Buddha suddenly come to life splashed with shafts of golden sunlight. Surrounding the temple are pillared cloister walls on which scenes from the two great Indian Epics, the *Ramayana* and the *Mahabharata*, are carved in deep relief. The stone canvas is over half a mile long and every inch is covered with exuberant action. Battles rage between demons and gods, elephants trample victims of spear and arrow. The fight continues on water and war canoes with

snake-headed prows thrust savagely at one another while their fighting men attack with sword and shield. Unfortunate losers flounder in the water where huge fish and crocodiles devour them.

There are also portraits of King Suryavarman II (1113–50), builder of Angkor Wat, the 'city temple'. Further on, giants and demons hoping to obtain the elixir of life churn the legendary sea of milk with Naga, the many-headed cobra king. Eventually, the legend tells, from the milky foam rose the celestial figures Devatas and Apsarases, whose beautiful forms are found in hundreds on the pillars and walls of Angkor.

Near the great Wat lie many other temples, each with its peculiar charm. Angkor Thom, the Bayon, Banteai Samre, Banteai Srei, Preah Khan all rising from the luxuriant green jungle, cool grey miracles of stone. Above, on every side, serene faces of the Buddha and Bodhisattva Avalokiteshvara, 'Lord of the World', gaze tranquilly down from their lofty towers on the sufferings of their builders. Their Mona Lisa smile suggests blissful meditation and a withdrawal from the wordly cares of the human race. Below, the courtyards and corridors swarm with the graceful dancing forms of Apsarases and Devatas. The greatest builder was King Jayavarman VII (1181–1220). He erected the Bayon, second in size only to Angkor Wat, as well as many monasteries and shrines. He was an ardent Buddhist, and like Ashoka was deeply concerned with the welfare of his people. He built over a hundred hospitals, and inscriptions of the time tell that he felt for the ills of his subjects more than for his own suffering.

The greatness of the Khmers lasted from the ninth to the fourteenth century. Little is known of their way of life. The forest swallowed this great civilization until 1861, when Henri Mouhot released the ruins from the grip of the jungle. These beautiful monuments witness the shortness of the life of power, but the Buddhism they represent lives on today in Cambodia as strongly as ever.

Above
Chinese ceramic figure of Kuan-yin, the Goddess of Mercy, seated on a lion.
Right
'The Laughing Buddha', a form of Maitreya, the Future Buddha.

Indonesia

The Khmers were greatly influenced by the culture of Java and Sumatra, now part of Indonesia. Buddhism was introduced to the Javanese during the second century A.D. by Indian merchants from Amaravati and Indonesian sculpture was influenced by work from this area as well as from Ajanta and Ellora. The finest flower of Indonesian Buddhism is the temple of Borobudur in Java. Here the Indonesians have injected the Indian forms with their own exuberance, giving them more warmth and humanity than their Indian counterparts. Indonesia is also responsible for the famous statue of Prajnaparamita, mother of all the Buddhas. This statue came from the Singhasari temple in eastern Java and is a masterpiece of Buddhist art. It is at present in the Rijksmuseum voor Volkenkunde, Leyden.

Laos and Vietnam

Further east Laos drew its cultural inspiration from Thailand and Cambodia, whilst Vietnam looked towards China and combined Mahayana Buddhism with ancestor worship, Taoism and Confucianism. The religions of these two small countries, with their long common frontier, face in opposite directions, one towards India and the west, the other towards China and the east. It was the meeting-place for the two great cultural zones of Buddhism and today is the battle-ground for the forces of communism and democracy.

This carved stone figure of Avalokiteshvara with eleven heads was made in China in the T'ang Dynasty (A.D. 618–907).

115

China

In China, after a struggle with the existing religion of Taoism, the philosophy of Confucianism and the teachings of Laotse, Buddhism finally became acceptable some three centuries after its arrival early in the Han dynasty about A.D. 64. Confucius, who, like Laotse and Gautama lived in the sixth century B.C., had confidence in the ultimate goodness and nobility of human nature. He believed that as the grass bends before the wind, so do the masses yield to the will of those above them. He argued therefore that, given a model ruler, a model people would forthwith appear. He would tell the ruling princes what they ought to do and from this would follow a kingdom filled with happy people who cared for their relatives and were well cared for themselves. Alas, none of the princes was liberal enough to accept his offer. This devotion to rule was illustrated when the State of Lu, where he was staying, fell into disorder and the ruler had to flee to the neighbouring State of Ch'i. Confucius left also as he would

The Bodhisattva Kuan-yin in this Chinese statue, of carved and painted wood, sits in the attitude of 'Royal Ease'. In Chinese art, Kuan-yin is sometimes masculine and sometimes feminine. Here, the sex is ambiguous but the softness of the modelling, particularly of the hands and face, suggests a feminine figure. Sung Dynasty, A.D. 960–1279.

Below
The threatening attitude of this Japanese carved-wood figure of a Guardian of the Faith fiercely proclaims that Buddhism will triumph over its enemies.

Below centre
As in other religions, Buddhism regards making a pilgrimage as evidence of an individual's piety. Many Buddhists travel long distances to visit holy places in order to have the satisfaction of making this act of devotion. Here, a thirteenth-century Japanese artist has attempted to convey something of a pilgrim's deep religious feeling in this carved and painted wood figure.

Below right
Figure of Maitreya (the 'Buddha to Be'). He is shown with one leg down as he rises from his cross-legged sitting position ready to descend to earth at the appointed time. China, sixth century A.D.

not countenance by his presence men who had driven out the legitimate ruler. On the way to Ch'i, Confucius and his disciples came upon a woman weeping at a grave. On being asked the cause of her grief, she replied that her father-in-law had been killed by a tiger, and also her husband and now her only son. When they asked why she did not leave such a dangerous place she said it was because there was no oppressive government. Confucius counselled his disciples to remember that an oppressive government is fiercer and more to be feared than a tiger.

Like Gautama, Confucius laid no claim to divine revelations. On being asked about life after death he replied, 'While you do not know life what can you know about death'; or again, 'While you cannot serve men, how can you serve spirits.' His 'golden rule' taught: 'What you do not like when done to yourself do not to others.'

The name Laotse means 'Old Philosopher'. He was born about 604 B.C. and he is the acknowledged founder of Taoism, that obscure mystical religion which has perhaps best been translated as 'The Way'. Like Buddhism it rejected all selfish approaches to life and held in great respect the virtues of gentle compassion, economy and humility. Before he died, Laotse left a small book called the *Tao-Te-Ching* of some 5,000 characters. In the closing chapter there is the following sentence: 'It is the way of Tao not to act from any personal

motive, to conduct affairs without feeling the trouble of them, to taste without being aware of the flavour, to account the great as small and the small as great, to recompense injury with kindness.' Like Buddhism, Tao is beyond the reach of word or definition, but those who possess it know its force and its beauty. It is the simplicity of action without motive, free from all selfish purpose, resting in nothing but its own accomplishment, like nature where plants spring up without words, fulfil their destinies without pride and give their fruits without assumption of ownership. The following poem was written before Laotse's death:

> 'Heaven is lasting and the earth enduring.
> The reason why they are lasting and enduring is that
> they do not live for themselves;
> Therefore they live long.
> In the same way the Sage keeps himself behind and
> he is in the front;
> He forgets himself and he is preserved.
> Is it not because he is not self-interested
> That his self-interest is established?'

It is easy to understand that with ideals already established and with the most advanced culture of that time in the world, the impact of Buddhism in China would progress only slowly. Gradually, over the centuries, the Taoist Way merged with the Eightfold Path, and in the T'ang Dynasty (618–906) Buddhism reached its greatest strength in China and produced with the native genius of the Chinese some of the finest art the world has known.

The Chinese speak of Buddhism and the doctrines of Laotse and Confucius as the Three Teachings. Together, they are the basis for all later Chinese thought, and a thorough knowledge of them is necessary for any real understanding between the East and West. These three teachings, of which Buddhism was the greatest and most profound, had common ground – they were all personal and tolerant. They pointed a Way, a Path, a Nobility, and were not doctrines of a church or a general rule. They were neither for nor against the existence and worship of the current gods. The Athenian philosophers had the same detachment; Socrates was quite willing to bow politely or sacrifice formally to almost any divinity. After drinking the hemlock he asked that a cock be sacrificed in the Temple of Asclepius as a thank-offering for his release from the long disease of living. While the intolerance towards other religions of the Christians, Jews or Moslems helped to preserve the essential faith of these communities, Buddhism had less effective methods of controlling the practices of the religions it sought to replace and so was weakened.

118

Above and below
The body of the Lord Buddha was identified in the scriptures as having 32 major and 80 minor marks. Some of these, such as the bulge on top of the head and the small disc between the eyes, are often shown in sculpture and painting, while others are frequently ignored.

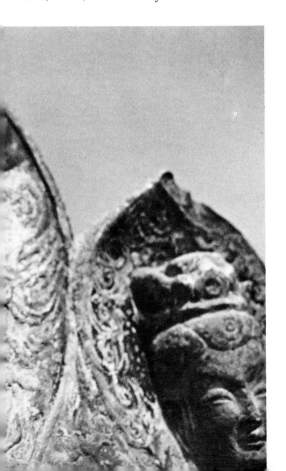

Japan and Zen

Above
Head of a Lohan; he is one of a group, often disciples of the Buddha, who have trodden the Eightfold Path and will escape rebirth when they pass into Nirvana after the death of their physical body. From Lung-men caves, China, sixth century A.D.

Buddhism came to Japan via Korea in A.D. 552. Up to that time the religious beliefs of the Japanese were based on the worship of their ancestors and of natural forces. They were an intelligent people, and when confronted by the highly developed form of Chinese Buddhism and a superior civilization, they quickly adopted the new pattern of thought. This was greatly helped by Prince Shotoku (574–622), the regent of the empire and one of the greatest men in the history of Japan. He was a contemporary of St Augustine of Canterbury and of Mahomet and had as much effect on his country as they had on theirs. He overcame the fierce resistance of the core of the Shinto cult and founded the Buddhist temple of Horyuji, built in 607 near Nara. This is the oldest Buddhist temple in Japan and has preserved the artistic treasure of the period, although its famous painted frescoes were destroyed by fire in 1949. Native craftsmen were taught by sculptors and artists from China and great shrines and temples were built throughout the country.

One of the most outstanding works of the later period is the colossal figure of Buddha Amida at Kamakura, erected in 1252. It is 42 feet high and the bronze cast weighs 210,000 pounds. The Buddha is seated in the posture of meditation representing the incarnation of Compassion, the spiritual principal of Buddha which was worshipped by the Pure Land School. There had been many schools of Buddhism in Japan. This is easily understandable since it was the last country in the East to receive the teaching and so received many different versions. Gradually the minor schools came together and by the time of the Kamakura period two main schools remained. The Pure Land School, which was simply a question of unreasoning faith, supplied the majority of the Japanese with what they required: a saviour Buddha who would save all who had faith and bring them to the paradise of the Pure Land. He was a Buddha of compassionate love and not a judge like the Christian God. But whilst the Pure Land School advised its followers to give up all attempts to find Enlightenment and to leave salvation to Buddha, to abandon the self to Buddha, Zen viewed the traditional aspects of Buddhism with hostility. Conventional scriptures, images and ritual were regarded with contempt and Zen sought to obtain Buddhahood by direct methods.

Zen was against theory and reasoning and desired direct insight rather than subtle thought. 'Don't think, try', was their motto. To argue over the scriptures, to meditate over words was regarded as a waste of time like studying sand in the desert. The goal of Zen is to see one's own nature, to know oneself; nothing else matters. Enlight-

119

enment comes in an all-revealing instant. The period of waiting may be an eternity, but Zen lays stress on the common mystical fact that enlightenment takes place in a timeless moment. It is not the gradual accumulation of merit that causes enlightenment, but a sudden act of recognition. It is a sudden leap from thinking to knowing. The mind of man is conditioned to considering and thinking about material that is already second-hand. It is a cage whose bars are the intellect. The senses are capable of direct experience; similar direct experience must be received by the intuition. The focal point is the iron curtain between the intellect and experience. This conflict is likened to the battle between reason and emotion which can never be won; both are enormously powerful but like the whale and the elephant they exist in different elements and are therefore unable to prevail upon or even meet one another. The purpose of Zen is to break down the bars of the intellect, to part the iron curtain and let the light from outside flood in. The question is where to begin, how to set about this formidable task. Words, as we have seen, are unable to explain the unexplainable, the appreciation of the infinite is beyond the capabilities of the finite mind. How then *does* one begin? Sometimes in childhood a sudden blinding wave of total happiness surges through the mind. 'Heaven' may indeed on rare occasions lie 'about us in our infancy'. The 'clouds of glory' still momentarily suffuse the newborn self. Such visions are not uncommon and Wordsworth expresses them beautifully and profoundly in his 'Ode on Immortality'.

Similar experiences may occur in later life: falling in love at first sight, when love for the loved one totally obliterates all thoughts of self; the sudden religious conversion, the seeing of the light which transforms men in an instant. Such happenings are rare and cannot be induced or indeed explained by words. The appreciation of Zen comes in an even higher degree, for once the hard shell of self is broken and the flood of light enters it remains for ever; the alteration is permanent. The purpose of Zen is to pass beyond the intellect. Just as the small vessel of Hinayana and the large vessel of Mayahana were constructed to help the followers of Buddha to cross the river of life, so Zen has devised a raft to try to help those unable to make the leap into direct awareness of themselves. The logs of the raft are any devices that will produce results and liberate men from their self-made prisons. All the scriptures and philosophies may be used, but once the far shore of enlightenment is reached the raft is abandoned. Two aids used by teachers of Zen are worth mentioning. The first is a series of rapid questions and answers between master and pupil which speed up the intellectual processes until they are suddenly transcended. The second is concentration on a phrase which can have no meaning to the intellect. It is easy to see the object of this attack on the intellect by words, but less easy to accept the nonsense that they make. Many examples are available and many arouse astonishment and hilarious laughter. Both these reactions are good for the spirit and greatly appreciated by teachers of Zen. Sudden enlightenment is the goal of

Zen; it is not the gradual accumulation of merit that causes enlightenment but a sudden act of recognition.

The falling of an apple made Newton instantly aware of the force of gravity. Gravity had always been present and so had Newton's ability to be aware, but it took the apple's fall to achieve realization. Zen techniques can be a sudden shock, a devastating experience, an explosion which bursts open the jam of logs in the river of the mind and lets all go free. These methods have been used since the fifth century by Zen. Today western psychiatrists also use shock treatment to relieve their patients.

The interest in Zen had a profound effect on the art of Japan. It produced a simplicity and purity of expression that has never been equalled in any other country. There arose a chastity of taste that forbade all embellishment. It is seen in the simple lines of the everyday porcelain, the cups and saucers used in the 'tea ceremony'; the ladle and the teapot are not only delicately beautiful in themselves but part of an exquisitely simple ceremony in which every act is part of a graceful sacrament. It is seen also in the elegant but stern lines of the buildings; in the exact placing and spacing of each stone and tree in the Japanese garden; in the lovely simple interiors of the Japanese home. Above all, the Japanese artist knew what to leave out, he was the master of uncluttered space, he knew more than anyone else the use of emptiness and of silence. The merest hint of form is sufficient. The beautiful paintings of bamboos which are so well known are the result of years of drawing bamboos until the artist is saturated with his subject; he then forgets the object and draws directly from his inspiration. The result is the absolute essence of bamboo. To Zen, nature and man are interwoven, the painter is in the picture, he is one with nature and nature with him.

Above
'The Great Sea' garden of the Daisen-in, Kyoto; the monk Soen Ozeki sits and contemplates the white expanse of raked sand.
Below
This Zen garden in the Ryoan-ji was probably designed in the mid fifteenth century A.D. It is made entirely of raked white sand and rocks, and may have been based on monochrome Chinese brush-and-ink paintings.

121

LONGING

Above
The delicate tracery of cast bronze forms part of a lantern which was made in about the eighth century A.D. It stands in the precinct of the Todai-ji, Nara, Japan.
Left
Amida is often called 'The Buddha of Boundless Light', which may make him distantly related to non-Buddhist gods of light such as those found in ancient Persia. He is popular in China, and also in Japan, where, as here, bronze figures of him are worshipped in the open air.

Longing to belong is a symptom of our age. The fragmented society of the West seeks security in great corporations, where the employees will be cared for from the cradle to the grave and will devote their lives to serving the interests of the company. Such sheltered lives – and many already exist – provide the individual with a sense of security, but it is the false kind of security that Gautama came to see through. Such communities become like the ant-heap, a teeming world where everything is subsidiary to the existence of the colony. The individual is expendable, for the continuity of the colony and the colony maintains its closed, unchanging existence as the ant-heap has done for over ten million years. Meantime man will soon have the challenge of leisure in abundance. Can he work out his own salvation or will his longing to belong drive him back to the wasted years of vanity and greed? An awakening Orient may once again revive interest in the deeper meaning of life.

Today Buddhism and Buddhist art have spread round the world, from Japan east to America, from India west to Europe. Except in China, Buddhism is on the increase, even in India, where the total number of Buddhists in 1951 was only 2,487, whilst in the 1961 census 3,250,227 were recorded. This was largely due to the caste system, which caused the downtrodden section of society to change to Buddhism where all men were equal and none untouchable.

In 1950 a World Fellowship of Buddhists was founded by Dr G. P. Malalesekera in Colombo, and since then congresses have been held every other year in different countries. But Buddhism does not produce organizers or secular leaders. Buddhists who dabble in politics degrade the Order and there can be no real head of a church where the whole endeavour is individual effort towards individual enlightenment. In the words of the Master, everyone must 'Work out his own salvation with diligence.'

Today science is challenging the finite quality of the human brain, a brain consisting of some 10,000 million electrically stimulated cells programmed with the instincts of our long history and receptive to new notions whether true or false. The aggregate of these cells provides our ever-changing personality, and their partial removal by surgery or altered rhythm by shock treatment changes our character. By such crude methods, aggression can be turned to fear, hatred to affection—how much better that they should be changed by appreciation of the realities that the philosophy of Buddha has placed in our hands!

The scientist cannot let his personal feelings come between him and the truth he is seeking; if he did he would be lost. The detective must consider the evidence objectively and impartially. The surgeon must operate without emotion or his skills would be blunted. But the majority of mankind still give free rein to their emotions, the

123

sincerity of their beliefs being taken as proof of their value. The burnings, the witch-hunts, the tortures of the Inquisition and the Gestapo, the innumerable examples of man's inhumanity to man, all spring from belief in an immortal self behind the self, of some indestructable person inside the body who guides the man in front to his terrible decisions. The primitive urge to kill is still accepted as part of everyday life, but those who betray humanity with false ideas and lead them to slaughter seldom survive long to enjoy their conquests.

The sabre-toothed tiger is extinct, but man's hair still rises in the presence of danger; his loves, hates, fears, angers, greeds and envies all spring from his struggle for survival. His clinging to self, a self which is only the bundle of experiences gathered on his long journey of life, is pointless. But like Pavlov's dog, he has been conditioned and is frightened to let go, even of that which in reality does not exist.

In the course of the next few years there will be an abundance of plenty for all mankind; the drudgery and slavery to maintain a bare existence are almost over. Science has already won the battle for a new world where the fruits of the earth will be sufficient for all and the universe will be a new playground. The key to this paradise lies in the wisdom of the great teachers, the narrow creed of selfish desire must give way to truth.

With the advance of science and psychology many of the older faiths have suffered. Their beliefs went against the new knowledge and the new knowledge won. But in this conflict the teaching of Buddha required no adjustments. Its wisdom has encompassed everything that modern thought can devise. Over 2,500 years ago the Buddhists had already solved many of the problems that modern psychology is still discovering. The man who told his followers to rely on nothing by faith but to test everything objectively and dispassionately had an approach to life which is in accordance with the best scientific tradition. The compassion and tolerance of his message makes it one which is acceptable to all.

It is perhaps significant that while mighty empires built upon greed and oppression have never lasted for more than a few centuries, the selfless life of the Buddhist community has carried it safely through 2,500 years. The meek have indeed inherited the earth. As the master said: 'Be ye lamps unto yourselves. Hold fast to the truth.'

Buddhist worship is often non-congregational since there is usually no need of priestly intercession. Worshippers, such as these outside the temple of Asakusa Kannon in Tokyo, go by themselves, or in small groups, to make their devotions whenever they feel the need to do so.

APPENDIX

BUDDHISM TODAY

Knowledge of Buddhism is being sought with increasing interest in the West, for it offers a personal philosophy to counteract the fragmented condition of Western society where many individuals no longer feel part of, or responsible for, the community in which they live. Expressions of this distress are seen in the demonstrations of students, flower people, hippies, and others who wish to drop out of, or change, a society which they feel no longer supplies their needs. For some the teachings of Buddha might provide a solution, but these are not easily absorbed by the Western mind, and to complicate matters there are a number of diverse schools, each with their own interpretation of the original doctrine. Efforts to find common ground have been made and one is included at the end of this appendix.

Divisions in the Order may have been foreseen by Buddha, when on his death-bed he declined to lay down any rules for the future and instead exhorted his followers to rely on themselves alone for guidance and not on any external help. However, it is in the nature of mankind to produce organizations, rituals, and rules, and beneath their administration the simple truths of the great teachers have, alas, on occasion been buried.

How then does an interested person approach Buddhism? Perhaps his best course would be to follow the example of Buddha and test the value of his Four Noble Truths and Eightfold Path, as he did himself by personal trial. The original teachings of Buddha have come down quite clearly through the ages, and he asks us to test them for ourselves. 'Work out your own salvation with diligence. Be ye lamps unto yourselves. Hold fast to the truth.' This truth must surely best be found by working it out in life by trial and error: a truth that grows out of our own living and thinking and not a dogma imposed from without. It may be that by being true to ourselves we shall find the way through life more simple and more rewarding.

TWELVE PRINCIPLES
OF BUDDHISM

1 Each human being is responsible for the consequence of his own thoughts, words and deeds. There is no Saviour, human or divine, who can give him enlightenment or prevent him attaining it. The purpose of life is to attain complete enlightenment, a state of consciousness in which all sense of separate selfhood is purged away. This purpose is fulfilled by treading the Eightfold Path, which leads from the 'house of self', aflame with hatred, lust and illusion, to the end of suffering for oneself and all beings.

2 The Buddha pointed out three Signs of Being. The first fact of existence is the law of change or impermanence. All that exists, from a man to a mountain, from a thought to a nation, passes through the same cycle of existence —birth, growth, decay and death. Life alone is continuous, ever seeking self-expression in new forms. This life-force is a process of flow, and he who clings to any form, however splendid, will suffer by resisting the flow.

3 The law of change applies equally well to the 'self'. There is no principle in an individual which is immortal and unchanging. Only the ultimate Reality, which the Buddha called 'The Unborn, Unoriginated, Unformed', is beyond change, and all forms of life, including man, are manifestations of this Reality. No one owns the life-force which flows in him any more than the electric lamp owns the current which gives it light. It is the foolish belief in a separate self, with its own selfish desires, which causes most of human suffering.

4 The universe is the expression of law. All effects have causes, and man's character is the sum total of his own previous thoughts, words and acts. Karma, meaning action-reaction, governs all existence, and man is the sole creator of his circumstances and his reactions to them, his future condition, and his final destiny. By right thought and action he can gradually purify his nature, and so attain in time liberation from rebirth. The process covers great periods of time, involving life after life on earth, but ultimately every sentient being will reach Enlightenment.

5 The life-force in which Karma operates is one and indivisible though its ever changing forms are innumerable and perishable. There is no death, save of temporary forms, but every form must pass through the same cycle of birth, growth, decay and death. From an understanding of life's unity arises compassion, a sense of identity with the life in other forms. Compassion is wisdom in action, a deep awareness of universal harmony. He who breaks this harmony by selfish action must restore it at the cost of suffering.

6 The interests of the part should be those of the whole. In his ignorance man thinks he can successfully strive for his own interests, and this wrongly-directed energy of selfish desire produces suffering. He learns from his suffering to reduce and finally eliminate its cause. The Buddha taught four Noble Truths: (a) the omnipresence of suffering; (b) its cause, wrongly-

The somewhat sensuous treatment of this Nepalese gilt-bronze figure of the goddess, 'the White Tara', contrasts paradoxically with the Buddhist renunciation of enjoyment gained from the senses.

directed desire; (c) its cure, the removal of the cause; and (d) the Noble Eightfold Path of self-development which leads to the end of suffering.

7 The Eightfold Path consists in Right (or Perfect) Views or preliminary understanding, Right Attitude of Mind, Right Speech, Right Action, Right Livelihood, Right Effort, Right Concentration or mind-development, and, finally, Right *Samadhi*, leading to full Enlightenment. As Buddhism is a way of living, not merely a theory of life, the treading of this Path is essential to self-deliverance. 'Cease to do evil, learn to do good, cleanse your own heart; this is the Teaching of the Buddha.'

8 The Buddha described the supreme Reality as 'the Unborn, Unoriginated, Unformed'. Nirvana, awareness of this Reality, is a state of Awakening (to the Truth within) or Enlightenment, and is the goal of the Eightfold Path. This supreme state of consciousness, the extinction of the limitations of self-hood, is attainable on earth. All men and all other forms of life contain the potentiality of Enlightenment, and the process therefore consists in consciously becoming what we already potentially are. 'Look within: thou *art* Buddha.'

9 From potential to actual Enlightenment there lies the Middle Way, the Eightfold Path 'from desire to peace', a process of self-development between the 'opposites', avoiding all extremes. The Buddha trod this Way to the end, and faith in Buddhism includes the reasonable belief that where a Guide has trodden it is worth our while to tread. The Way must be trodden by the whole man, not merely the intellect, and Compassion and Wisdom must be developed equally. The Buddha was the All-Compassionate as well as the All-Enlightened One.

10 Buddhism lays stress on the need of inward concentration and meditation, which leads in time to the development of the inner spiritual faculties. The subjective life is as important as the daily round, and periods of quietude for inner activity are essential for a balanced life. The Buddhist should at all times be 'mindful and self-possessed', refraining from mental and emotional attachment to the things and occasions of daily life. This increasingly watchful attitude to circumstance, which he knows to be his own creation, helps him to keep his reaction to it always under control.

11 The Buddha said: 'Work out your own salvation with diligence.' Buddhism knows no authority for truth save the intuition of the individual, and that is authority for himself alone. Each man suffers the consequences of his own acts, and learns thereby, while helping his fellow men to the same deliverance; nor will prayer to the Buddha or to any God prevent an effect from following its cause. The utmost tolerance is practised towards all other religions and philosophies, for no man has the right to interfere in his neighbour's journey to the Goal.

12 Buddhism is neither pessimistic nor 'escapist'. It is a system of thought, a religion, a spiritual science and a way of life, which is reasonable, practical and all-embracing. For 2,500 years it has satisfied the spiritual needs of nearly one third of mankind. It appeals to those in search of truth because it has no dogmas, satisfies the reason and the heart alike, insists on self-reliance coupled with tolerance for other points of view, embraces science, religion, philosophy, psychology, mysticism, ethics and art, and points to man alone as the creator of his present life and sole designer of his destiny.

(These Twelve Principles of Buddhism are reproduced here with the kind permission of the Buddhist Society, London)

TECHNICAL DATA

CAMERAS: Two Nikon F Photomic Tn; one Nikkormat FT.

LENSES: Nikkor Auto 28mm F 3.5, 35mm F 2.8, 50mm F 2; Micro Auto 55mm F 3.5, 105mm F 2.5, 200mm F 4.

All lenses fitted with lens hoods and protected with UV filters. Colour and neutral density filters were also used. Film stock used was Kodachrome 2 and Kodak Tri-X – they were given normal exposure at meter reading with shutter speeds of usually 125th of a second or faster. Flash was supplied by two Mecablitz 163 with mains charging units.

FURTHER READING

E. CONZE, *Buddhism, its Essence and Development.*

E. CONZE, *A Short History of Buddhism.*

A. FOUCHER, *The Life of the Buddha.*

Sir EDWIN ARNOLD, *The Light of Asia.*

D. T. SUZUKI, *The Essence of Buddhism.*

D. SECKEL, *The Art of Buddhism.*

Sir JOHN MARSHALL, *The Buddhist Art of Gandhara.*

B. P. GROSLIER, *Angkor.*

W. WILLETTS, *Chinese Art.* (2 vols.)

P. C. SWANN, *An Introduction to the Arts of Japan.*

CHRISTMAS HUMPHREYS, *Buddhism.*

PAUL CARUS, *The Gospel of Buddha.*

CREDITS

The following institutions and individuals all helped to make this book and its range of illustrations possible by the facilities and courtesies they extended:

Amsterdam: Museum van Aziatische Kunst (Rijksmeum). Birmingham: City Museum and Art Gallery. Boston: Museum of Fine Arts. Calcutta: Indian Museum. Lahore: Central Museum. Leiden: Rijksmuseum voor Volkenkunde. London: British Museum; Victoria and Albert Museum. Moscow: State Museum of Oriental Art. New Delhi: National Museum. New York: Metropolitan Museum of Art. Paris: Musée Cernuschi; Musée Guimet. Washington: Freer Gallery of Art. Berlin: Staatliche Museen, Museum für Indische Kunst.

S. Hayashida, Director of Japan Information Centre, London. Y. Odaka, Chief Overseas Public Relations Officer, Tokyo. Professor Ichiro Suzaki, Director of Kokusai Bunka Shinkokai, Tokyo. Dr Hurusawa, Director of the Tokyo Botanic Garden. Mr Jiro Fumoto, Director of the Botanic Garden, Kyoto. Dr Hideo Kato, Director of the Kokusai Bunka Shinkokai, Kyoto. Mr Koichi Yoko, Director of the Kokusai Bunka Shinkokai, Nara.

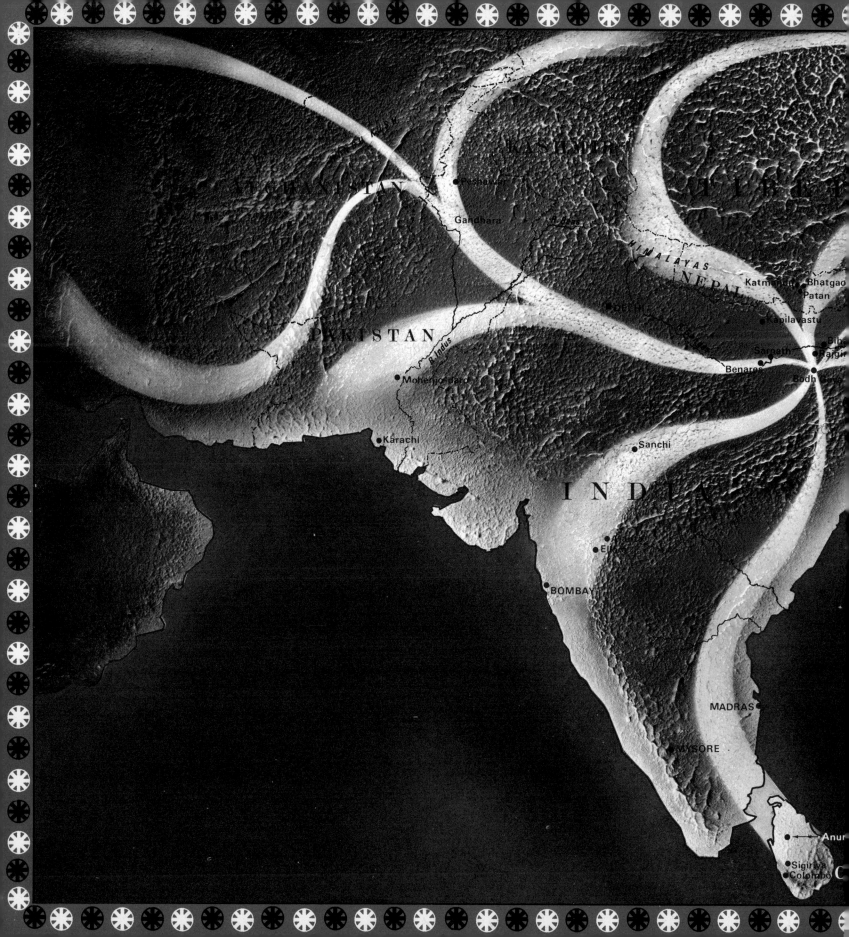